The Joy
of Money

PAULA NELSON

The Joy
of Money

*The guide to
women's financial
freedom*

𝔰𝔡

STEIN AND DAY/*Publishers*/New York

First published in 1975
Copyright © 1975 by Paula Nelson
All rights reserved
Designed by Ed Kaplin
Printed in the United States of America
Stein and Day/*Publishers*/Scarborough House,
Briarcliff Manor, N.Y. 10510

Library of Congress Cataloging in Publication Data

Nelson, Paula, 1945-
    The Joy of money.

      1.   Finance, Personal.   2.   Saving and thrift.
3.   Investments—United States.   4.   Women in business.
I.   Title.
HG179.N422   332′.024   75-9847
ISBN 0-8128-1816-4

For Peter
and all that we have shared

ACKNOWLEDGMENTS

To George Otis for the *spark,* Jean Rejaunier for the *lead,* George O'Neil for an important *hello,* Arthur Abelman for the *literary link;* Julie Fallowfield for the *British interview,* Hap Heyden for the *11th-Hour Peptalk,* Peter Stanton for his *understanding,* and Pat Myrer for always believing.

And, my special thanks to Dr. Tessa Albert-Warschaw, Carol Sapin Gold, Jean Williams, Shirley Chilton, Richard Gibson, Julie Stomne, Marion Shuster, Pat Martin, Nancy Boxley Tepper, Steve Campbell, Maggie Waite, Joe Burdett, Pete Stanton, Jr., Porter Hendricks, Gayle Hannifious, Cheri Cole, and my parents, Rose and Clinton Nelson.

Contents

proof of financial competence. Establishing your
credit rating with banks. The new credit law. How
to select the bank and branch most helpful to you.
How to cultivate your banker. The importance of a
bank account in your own name. Start at the top.

Banker. Lawyer. Stockbroker. CPA/Tax Accountant.
Real Estate Broker. Insurance Agent. How to find and
select these top-flight pros. How to define your need.
How to hire the *right* professional to fill it. The important face-to-face interview. Seven crucial points to
remember before making dispassionate and wise
choices. Asking the right questions. Make the pros
work for *you*.

Building the confidence to move from the routine to
the challenging. The most exciting thing about running your own company. "Not everyone is cut out to
be boss." Take a hard look at your motivations. Evaluating a corporation. Women who made it. "Happiness is competence fullfilled." Are you being held back
in your job? Being the best. Seven essential qualities to
help you achieve "the pure joy of winning."

Make a clear blueprint—*in advance*. "Will it work?
How will it work? Will you make any money out of
it?" Your business plan or "money presentation" has
wide uses. A selling tool for many purposes. A scenario
for your future and what you can accomplish. Know
what the market is and how to tap it. A simple marketing plan. How to draw up your earnings forecast.

Working with your banker. Debt financing vs. equity

financing. Office expenditures—pitfalls and necessities. Accountants. Incorporating vs. partnership. "What is a business going to be worth?" Creative thinking: "Businesses within businesses." Spin-offs and franchises. Seek advice: suppliers, bankers, distributors, educators. "A good image must be earned by performance."

The fine art of negotiation. Hitting the boss for a raise: your four-point game plan. Establishing your position. "The third party ploy." The bargaining game: credibility, psychology and maneuver, fallback positions. Rehearsal for the drama of negotiation. "Preparation is the key to success."

Getting your money to start working for *you*. The financial adviser—pros and cons. "Hot tips—the midway shell game." Building Your Financial Planning Pyramid. Insurance—shield and hedge. Retirement plans. Your investment spectrum: from savings accounts to commercial paper. How to *really* beat inflation. "Running aggressive money." How do you know what company is worthy of investment? How to read a financial report. Assets and liabilities. Six points on analyzing corporate health. Be adventurous—and informed.

Wall Street: the market *is* a woman's world, too. "Common sense can get you there." How to pick the *right* stockbroker. Seek a range of opinion. Penetrating questions to ask. Use the interview to advantage. Selecting the stocks for your pocketbook. Making a habit of being practical and objective. How to research your stocks. Stockholders' meetings and how they work. Investment clubs.

freedom and responsibility. "Staying power"—name of the real estate game. "Raw" land vs. improved land. "Leverage." Group investment in recreational areas. Apartment house management—tax shelter, hedge against inflation. "Fix-up property." Escrow, compensating balances, capital gains. Commercial and industrial property—the big money. Three basic rules for land purchase.

Coping successfully with taxes. "What you don't understand can cost you money." Use the IRS. Your tax accountant. The difference between legal avoidance and illegal evasion. Plotting your tax course *in advance*. Capital gains and losses: "Never sell a security to get a tax break." Deductions for investors. Types of returns. IRS audits: what to do if you are called. Gifts and estate taxes. Trusts. "Anticipating is the watchword."

The Joy
of Money

1 /

Women and the
Money Mystique

I had noticed her in the audience while I was still speaking: a slender, beautifully groomed woman in her mid-thirties. She looked remarkably like Joanne Woodward: the warmth, the vulnerability, the steady, eager gaze. I've forgotten her name, but I'll never forget what she said to me.

A break followed my part of the financial seminar. That was when she came up and introduced herself. "I just want to shake your hand," she murmured, "because what you're saying is so important." I was pleasèd, and a little flattered, until she said:

"My marriage has just broken up after fifteen years. My two girls are nine and seven, and I don't even know how much my husband is worth—or what we had in the bank or anywhere else."

In that simple admission she threw into high relief everything I'd been trying to say that evening. She wasn't yet seeking answers to the complex questions of inflation or investments. This was something far more fundamental—and frightening. There she stood, Ms. America: pretty and bright and self-assured. But in terms of money—its power, its pitfalls, its boundless potential for joy and self-fulfillment—she was crippled.

"I simply assumed it was *his* role to take care of everything," she went on. "Checking accounts, savings and stocks and things like that. We had our problems, but money was always in the middle of it. You know, it's just dawned on me—maybe my attitude about money was the last straw. I see now it's up to *me* to put my own house in order."

Listening to her, I thought: If I could have talked with this woman last year . . . If someone had only talked with *me* ten years ago . . .

I remembered something I'd read in Lyn Caine's deeply moving, candid bestseller, *Widow*.

"Money matters," she learned shortly after her husband's death. "It really does. It's right up there with love and security and identity."

Her husband, a bankruptcy attorney, had left their financial affairs "in a terrible mess." Ms. Caine was suddenly confronted with the problem of supporting herself and their two children. She and her husband had never discussed finances.

It was just one of those unliberated things, I suppose, going back to the idea that little girls aren't good at math, a self-fulfilling prophecy that encourages financial incompetence. The fact that I never shared any of the real responsibilities. . . . Why should any woman face deprivation and financial terror because her husband dies? Women must . . . stop playing child/wife. That role hasn't been valid for a long time.

Another victim of the Great American Shell Game was Doris Day. Despite a fabulously successful career, she found her financial affairs in a shambles after the death of her husband and business manager, Martin Melcher. Like so many other women, Ms. Day had entrusted the handling of her money to her husband. Melcher, in turn, gave over the management of their joint finances—and control of the millions of dollars his wife had earned—to *his* lawyer and business manager, Jerome Rosenthal.

"I was so busy working at the time, I really didn't know what was going on," Ms. Day explained. "I couldn't be at the office and the studio, too." Her suit against Rosenthal for fraud and malpractice resulted in the awarding of more than $22 million to Ms. Day. The judgment is currently under appeal, but Ms. Day's suit against her ex-lawyer was a giant step toward financial responsibility. Her case again affords dramatic evidence that you put your economic future in the hands of others at your peril. Money must become your second vocation, as Ms. Day has realized.

Unhappily, stories like these abound—and not just among widows and divorcees. Single and married women also too often discover that "nothing stings more deeply than the loss of money." It's true that the irrevocable power of money to change one's life often makes itself felt most when a woman is divorced or widowed, when she receives or is deprived of money. Then it becomes personal, a direct and consuming influence. But all women feel the impact of money each moment of their lives, whether they realize it or not.

Why write a money book for women? One might rightfully assume that no distinction should be made between the sexes, but let's face reality: Women's battle for financial equality has barely been joined, much less won. Society still traditionally assigns to woman the role of money-handler rather than money-maker, and our assigned specialty is far more likely to be home economics than financial economics. While our power in the consumer area is accepted, that's a small serving indeed from the financial feast—and it's been a dreary sop for entirely too long.

Women own 75 percent of America's stocks and bonds and 65 percent of its savings accounts. But the statistics are misleading, for two reasons: First, we live longer than men, which pushes these figures out of proportion. Second, we may own most of the nation's wealth, but we don't control it. It's most often held in our names—in pension funds, trust funds, insurance policies, all of which in turn are controlled or handled by other people. *Control* is where the real action is. And the fun.

What has kept us from the fun of making rather than just spending or handling money? From the satisfaction that genuine financial responsibility inevitably brings?

Education and indoctrination are obvious villains. Those grade-school readers, complete with illustrations, that used to say: "Here is the father, bringing home the money." "Here is the mother, paying out the money." The tendency, still with us in many school systems, is actively to discourage girls from taking an interest in mathematics, economics, finance.

Consider today's intelligent woman, gazing apprehensively at the money-hydra with its thousand heads. It's easy enough to put the blame on her education, but that isn't the whole story. The problem runs deeper. Between woman's appointed societal role and her achievement of financial success lies a barrier so effective that it kept us passively accepting the role of money moron for centuries: the money mystique, based on the myth that financial expertise is distinctly unfeminine.

Money, so the myth goes, is a man's game in that man's world out there, and women needn't worry their pretty little heads about it. "O frailty, thy name is woman," and all that jazz. Forget it. Women themselves have always known that they have good sense, and it is now apparent that, despite the money mystique, many women have managed to break out of this Medieval financial type casting. They *are* worrying their heads about money—some of them to spectacular effect, as these pages will show. And their success has exploded the myth of the money mystique.

The idea that the female brain is somehow too feeble to grasp the intricacies of the business world dies at the hands of women like a group of nine who, in the early 1970s, handled a $50,000 fund bequeathed to Scripps College with the stipulation that it was to be managed solely by women students. At the outset, none of the women had any experience in the financial area.

For three months the nine of them studied the stock market, talked with brokers, pored over publications like the *Wall Street Journal*. They then entered the stock market—at a point when it was declining. In six months they increased the fund's worth by 10 percent. Which, you may rest assured, showed a far better track record than many professional money managers were achieving just then.

The making of money simply is not a sex-linked skill. Women can and are turning it all around. We are discovering for ourselves the challenge—and the joy—of money.

•

"Honey, I've been rich and I've been poor," Pearl Bailey used to say. "And rich is better."

Right on, Pearl. Nobody ever put it better. The joy of money can be as sweet as the joy of life, for it can bring you life's most abundant gifts, and the leisure to enjoy them. Money *is* time. Wisely governed, it opens a thousand doors to enrich our lives and to enable us, in turn, to enrich the world around us. Money is more than security, it is your passport to independence, to power, to control of your own future.

Money-making is also an art—an art to take pride in. Creativity, a concept not often associated with the making or managing of money, *should* be. What should not be associated with money-making is terms like "money-grubbing," which convey the notion that nice people, particularly women, don't concern themselves with "vulgar" money. (We should all know by now that nice people make money right and left!) Happily, as you will see, women are bringing their particular creative skills as never before to every aspect of the financial scene.

Making *real* money depends upon your ability to become financially self-assertive. Until your creative energy is freely directed toward productive financial channels, you won't become independent. Saving small amounts of money or living on a budget simply won't do the trick. When you limit your financial horizons to careful consumerism, you are limiting a financial potential that could be boundless. The intelligent investor, woman or man, learns that risks, thoughtfully taken, can become constructive gains. Think big—but be sure you think!

You may be intelligent, you may have uncommon ability to make others see things your way, you may have ease of manner, charm, self-assurance. But none of these qualities will significantly change your financial prospects until *you* summon the will and knowledge to put it all together. You can make money work creatively for you if first you become creative in your own thinking about money. At the outset, it will take a lot of hard work, ruthless self-examination, and disciplined observation of the ground rules. It then takes courage and imagination to make your first flight and to maintain altitude. Be resilient and flexible; be open to new ideas. You will enjoy a kind of pride in having developed your competence in money matters, and you will find that the rewards accompanying that pride can be spectacular.

Once you've set your course for financial liberation, once you've assessed where your best talents lie and how much you can realistically hope to achieve—most of all, once you have built the confidence to conquer your fear of the money world—you will be free to respond to its exciting challenges. Once you're able to cope with flair and distinction in big and small ways, you will find the money game the best game in town. Here we're playing for keeps. And the stakes are your future.

My own financial education was anything but traditional. While many people are introduced to the money world through their own personal finances or through college economics courses, I slipped in through the side door of corporate finance. At the time, I actually knew more about corporate underwritings and the stock market than how to keep my checkbook straight.

Ten years ago, at the age of nineteen, I started working for a small aerospace manufacturing company which was headed by a successful entrepreneur and financial wizard complete with an MBA from Harvard, Peter Stanton. The economy at the time was very definitely in a go-go mood, and much of the talk around me was geared to when the Dow-Jones Industrial Average would break 1,000. (Broadway even had a hit entitled *How Now, Dow Jones.*) I enjoyed a fascinating introduction to the business world—I'd have had to have been deaf, dumb, and blind not to have caught some of the electricity in the financial air those days.

I learned a lot simply by osmosis: looking and listening,

and reading *The Wall Street Journal*, which even then I found a kind of off-beat status symbol for certain women. Since the company I had joined was small, I was able to sit in on many of the financial meetings and watch the decision-making process at work.

Anyone who tries to tell you that financial meetings aren't "power sessions" hasn't attended many. It is a simple truth that money is power, and power correctly wielded can yield an uncommon satisfaction. In fact, while I then still hadn't yet made the connection between the sense of excitement I felt and my own participation in the exercise of power I now realize how much a part that very sensation played in attracting me to the business world. Henry Kissinger was once quoted as saying that "power is the ultimate aphrodisiac." I don't know about that, but I *have* felt the sheer exhilaration of effective decision-making, of winning my way to financial independence through my own efforts. I was suddenly where the power was. And I knew it.

After a time the glow wore off, to be replaced by a more serious attitude. I had decided to become a businesswoman; and though I knew I'd stumbled into the world of business and finance by a lucky accident, I was determined to stay in that world by design.

What followed this sober decision was the Paula Nelson Financial Education Program. I attended seminars offered by stockbrokers. I learned that, given due study, their jargon was perfectly comprehensible, and I began piecing together a rudimentary understanding of some of the basics on which the business and financial worlds rest. Perhaps my greatest asset at the time was my carefree naïveté: I felt perfectly able to ask the most elementary questions without worrying whether someone might think me stupid. Asking questions and listening to the replies are as important in finance as in anything else.

During this period the aerospace company was sold and I joined forces with Peter Stanton and an electronics engineer in a new venture. It was called Infonics, Inc., and I took charge of its sales and marketing program. In three years,

Infonics, a manufacturer of tape-copying equipment, grew from a fledgling three-person company into a million-dollar corporation; a Los Angeles newspaper reported in a four-column spread that "Paula Nelson has increased the company's sales by 400 percent in two-and-a-half years. She supervises a home office staff ... does business with 100 dealers she has established in the United States, and has now set up 24 distributors abroad."

It was obviously an exciting time for me—in fact, it seemed that I could do no wrong. The crowning moment came in 1969, when Infonics had a public stock issue and the stock climbed from $5 a share to more than $26. So did the value of the stock option I had obtained when the company was founded.

For many of us, money beomes real all at once, without any advance warning. It did for me, when I recognized the dollar worth of a stock option I held, and the fact that it now represented a potential source of financial independence. For another woman that moment may come after an inheritance or a divorce settlement. However it comes, for the first time she sees money as "*my* money."

But money that isn't supported by adequate knowledge and planning can vanish almost as suddenly as it appeared. It's one thing to carve out a corporate niche for yourself, earn a handsome salary, and capitalize on a stock option, and quite another to assume the responsibility of seizing the financial opportunity that your income and position have made possible.

Like many single women, I found I was floating in a kind of economic holding pattern, waiting for someone to come along and take charge of that part of my life. It was *A Doll's House* all over again. I was a 1960s career executive, and a good one, but in terms of my personal finances I was acting like a nineteenth-century hausfrau. Financial responsibility, I finally saw, is every individual's problem and opportunity. If I evaded either, I would have to accept whatever I was handed. And that I didn't want.

It was time to shift gears, to grow up. I decided that money must, in a very real sense, become my "second vocation"—that is, if I was to keep any of my nest egg and not be forever dependent on a nine-to-five job (no matter how much it paid) and the whim of management.

The big question was where to begin. My first thought was to turn the entire kit and kaboodle over to a financial adviser, but that idea quickly fizzled when I learned that the best money managers have little interest in accounts under $100,000. I then talked with friends and associates. Dozens of enthusiastic schemes were presented to me, from olive groves to oil wells. Many people insisted that the stock market was the only place to make any *real* money. I came away horrified by my own ignorance and that of most of my friends. I had gained a mishmash of contradictory information, half-baked plans, and precious few of the hard facts I was looking for on which to build a secure financial foundation. That was when I decided to sit down with my yellow pad and pencil, and use the same logic that I had always used in business.

And it worked.

The first step was assembling a financial photograph in order to find out exactly what I was worth. This was a refreshing exercise, since I found I had more to work with than I had realized.

Next, I set down my immediate financial goals and sketched a plan of action for the next twelve months. And then I brainstormed, letting my imagination roam free, while tempering it with a sense of hard reality, in order to develop a five-year plan. Yes, five whole years ahead.

The third step was determining what financial tools I needed to achieve my five-year goal. I had learned through experience that certain top professionals, be they brokers, lawyers, bankers, or accountants, are indispensable in the business world. I needed to know how to go about selecting these professionals, how to develop the art of asking the right questions in order to determine whether a particular investment was right for me.

My final step was to define what I thought of as my "visibility profile": specifically, which options were open and available to me, in harmony with my interests and skills, within my reach. I've found that many people wander around wearing financial blinders, looking at only one small corner of the money world. In fact, the options for making money and investing it are virtually limitless—and therein lies both an opportunity and a problem. Early on in my career I thought the only royal road to riches was through the stock market; but I soon realized it was only one option, and by no means the right one for everyone.

The point is a crucial one: If you are to achieve success in the financial world, you must discover where *your* true interests and talents lie. Then dig in, dig deep, and specialize in that area. What excites you? Is it the stock market? Real estate? Art or antiques? Commodities, gold, or beef, or cotton futures? Or do you long to launch your own company, however small?

Everyone comes to the question of skills and interests with a different supply of emotional and financial resources, and the decision is consequently a very personal one. It is vital, nonetheless. An astute choice—for you—can be rewarding indeed. Only after I had put together my own profile could I begin the creative process of effective money-managing.

The era of the knowledgeable, competent woman in business has already begun. The big breakthroughs have been made. It may be unusual (it is mighty unusual!) to earn a staggering six-figure salary like Barbara Walters, but the $20,000-to-$30,000-a-year range is a readily attainable goal. Today women of any age need no longer wait for a financial Prince Charming. More and more we are looking to ourselves, to our newly aroused consciousness of the role that money can and should play in our lives. We also know it is unfair—yes, *unfair*—for men to carry the burden of total financial responsibility alone: Many men are simply not equipped for it. Women today have proved we can pull our financial weight, and we intend to keep right on doing so with a new spirit of confidence. We've found that the biggest obstacle toward realizing that "second vocation" is the fear of failure—or success. We've even found out how much fun it can be.

I have experienced my own "financial awareness evolution," and I know the rewards that come with it. I also know that it doesn't happen overnight and cannot happen in a vacuum. This book will not offer effortless shortcuts to boundless riches, or guarantee that you will become a millionaire in two years. The reason for that is simple: I don't believe there *are* any easy shortcuts. I do believe that the shortest route to your financial freedom lies in knowing yourself, knowing what you need to do to achieve your goals, and realizing that those goals can be achieved. Once you accept your own financial responsibility, achieve your own definable economic goals, that's when making money can provide a new dimension to your life.

If you're single, you can enjoy not only the pleasures money can bring—we all like skiing at St. Moritz or swimming off Sardinia—but the deeper excitement of having your own ability create for you a lasting freedom. If you're married, you and your husband can experience the pleasure of working toward the fulfillment of common goals. Money is too important to be the source of bickering. It's one of the realities of life. Face it and enjoy it.

When I asked a young California businesswoman, Carol Sapin Gold, how she would rate the importance of money on a scale of one to ten, her reply was simple and direct: "Eleven."

This is not to suggest that you become obsessed by money. Any obsession is boring, and a subject as fascinating as money should never become a bore. Money is indeed a good servant and a bad master. What I'm speaking for is freedom—the freedom money can bring, the opportunity to expand your horizons, the chance to do what you really want to do with your life.

Creatively pursued, money can work for you, grow for you, and help you to find the unique excitement of shaping and controlling your own future. As I hope you will discover, *that's* the real joy of money.

2 /

Goals: You *Can*
Get There from Here

We had scheduled the interview for the hour following our joint seminar at the Ambassador Hotel in Los Angeles. Carol Sapin Gold has been called dynamic and personable, and the word "talented" inevitably comes up, too. Three years ago she decided to launch her own company, specializing in communications and personnel relations, working as a consultant in designing training programs. Since opening day three years ago, she has worked with an impressive number of blue-chip companies (these are in fact the only ones she works with), including IBM, Jet Propulsion Labs (Cal Tech), and Datsun, to name only a few.

My first question was: "What do you consider the key element in your business success?"

Carol doesn't just answer a question, she envelops it.

"I'm a goal-setter," she said. "I establish goals in order to separate the wheat from the chaff, so I can zero in on what I really want. Once I set a goal for myself, I can visualize myself doing it, and then I can go back and work out how to get there on a step-by-step basis. Then I go into immediate action. It isn't an overnight process.

"I'll give you an example. When I decided to start my company, I was phasing out of my position at Great Western Financial, and with their approval I used that phase-out time to wrap up three major consulting contracts, get my stationery and cards printed, order my business phone. When January second dawned and everything was in place, I was in business. I had targeted my goal, planned how to achieve it—and I had the pleasure of realizing that accomplishment. I look at goals as a kind of personal road map. They give me direction so I can concentrate on what's truly important, and I use them in business as well as in my personal life.

"Goals create energy, because suddenly your energy can be directed in one channel instead of flowing in twenty undefined directions. I've never met a successful person who doesn't use goals."

Another firm believer in goals is Shirley Chilton, who rose from a position as switchboard operator to become chairman of the board of Daniel Reeves and Company, a member of the New York Stock Exchange headquartered in Los Angeles.

"I've made goals for myself ever since childhood," she told me. "When I was nine, my goal was to become the best student I possibly could and I ended up being valedictorian of my class. Ever since then I've set short-term and long-term goals and tried my best to achieve each of them within a certain period of time. This is every bit as important after you've won a certain position as before. Right now I'm planning what I'll do after I retire."

Read that last sentence again. That's the most significant thing about Shirley's grand design: She has gone far beyond the typical one-year or five-year goal—she has a *life plan*. Whereas most of us entertain some fantasies about spending our retirement gardening or traveling, Shirley knows exactly what she wants and has already begun preparing for it: She's going to be writing children's books that deal with economics and how our free enterprise system works. She has begun preparing for this new career (easily twenty years away) by publishing a series of four books that she wrote in collaboration with her husband, F. Roy Chilton, and her son Robert.

Once you've decided to achieve your own financial freedom, you must, from the start, define your financial goals. This means asking yourself some intriguing questions. What, specifically, is your own particular long-range money goal? Do you want to be rich—really rich? Or do you simply want to have enough money so that you need never worry about not having as much as you want?

Would you enjoy a life of leisure on three continents? Or does the idea of international business travel turn you on? Do you want to own and run your own company? Or would you prefer the security of a high salary with a major company, living on a certain income that won't be seriously threatened by inflation or by shifts in the economy?

Perhaps your long-range goal involves a combination of some or all of the above—or none of the above. Whatever it is, you'll need to decide *at the outset*. Then you'll be ready to get down to shorter-term goal strategy.

Goals need to be established in at least three time chunks: short-term (one year), intermediate (three years), and long-term (five years). Actually pinpointing a dollar goal is often extremely difficult, but it can be done and it is absolutely vital. If you're an excellent planner like Shirley Chilton, you might work at developing a twenty-year or life plan. But initially these three phases covering five years are adequate. Most people, once they've developed goals, tend to get hooked on them for one simple reason: They work.

Here are my own suggestions for financial goal planning:

1. *Write your goals down, or type them up.* You need to pin yourself down on this: It's your visible, tangible commitment.

2. *Keep your goals high, but realistic.* Billie Jean King worked and willed herself to become a great tennis champion—and then used that position to become publisher of a women's sports magazine. She didn't try to become a film star or a foreign affairs adviser to the president. She knew where her field of excellence lay, and she moved, very successfully, within that framework. Your financial goals must be guided by the same healthy practicality. Obviously, planning to buy in the near future property worth $100,000 on an annual income of $15,000 is anything but realistic.

3. *Always set a time frame in which to achieve a goal.* A

promotion in one year, say; or owning your own firm in three years; or an annual salary of $25,000 in five years. This will not only enable you to keep a watchful eye on your progress, it will also force you to ask yourself some more hard questions (which is even more to the good). Are you being paid enough in your present job? Does your employer place an adequate value on your talents? Above all, are you drifting in your current job, just doing what has to be done without developing a sense of direction?

4. *Establish mini-goals as stepping-stones to major goals and quantify them in terms of the time and money (if any) required to achieve them.* Setting minimal goals in themselves—telling yourself you'll take this if you can't have that, and then you'll be satisfied—is obviously self-defeating. Minimal goals are every woman's great pitfall: Don't fall for them. When Helen Gurley Brown took over the editorship of *Cosmopolitan*, her presumed goal was to get the magazine back on the profitable side of the ledger. Instead of aiming at a general readership, she selected one market she knew a great deal about, the single girl, and set flat-out to capture it. The circulation figures, advertising, and balance sheets of *Cosmo* demonstrate that she was right in focusing on one specific market—but with the larger goal always in view.

5. *Change your goals when your circumstances change.* Remember that rules are made to be broken, when occasion demands. Review your progress in ninety days, or six months. Don't make rules for yourself so rigid that they can't be changed or achieved. Money is probably the most fluid commodity in the world today (as the following chapters will show), and you need to keep your program flexible, even as you keep your overall effort consistent.

6. *Take immediate action.* Don't procrastinate on this. This is the most important point of all. "Opportunity once forsaken is opportunity lost forever," as Omar Bradley, the celebrated "GIs' general," put it, and that's every bit as true in the world of business. There's a niche for you out there in real estate or electronics or corporate finance, but you'll never fill it if you

sink back into the nine-to-five syndrome, or wait for manna from heaven, or go around murmuring to yourself, "This job will do until I get married." Says economist Peter Drucker: "The future will not just happen if one wishes hard enough. It requires decision—now. It imposes risk—now. It requires action—now." Set it out on a sheet of paper:

FINANCIAL GOALS

Goal	*$ Cost*	*Date Begun*	*Achievement Date*

The key to creating and defining your goals is the quality and depth of a personal question-and-answer session. You have to face yourself first. Then, if you are developing a family financial goal, you should work closely with your husband and your older children. Raise *their* financial consciousness, for they ought to be an integral part of the effort and achievement. I'm not talking about budget meetings, but horizon sessions. They can be fun—and productive.

My own family was involved in land and real estate. Some of my early memories are of sitting with my parents across the desk from Donna Swink, head of the escrow department at the Santa Monica Bank. I remember listening to the discussions, watching everyone go through and sign the papers, seeing the checks exchanged. Occasionally I went along with my parents to talk to real estate people. I saw houses bought and sold, and once when I was nine and my parents were out I showed a house to some interested buyers. I simply mimicked all the things I'd heard my mother say, even discussing the terms of payment! I've always felt that I was lucky to have this kind of early exposure. It's probably the reason it's been easier for me to be free of much of the fear of the financial world that has gripped so many women.

Back to goals: It's important to open up your mind and allow yourself creative dreaming in the course of developing your goals. What do I want to be, where do I want to be? How much do I want to be worth? However, it's equally important for that creative dreaming to evolve into a concrete, reasonable, step-by-step plan. If the dream won't conform, drop that one and try another.

Here are fifteen questions that will help you start the thinking process:

1. Are you currently engaged in a career?
2. Are you considering changing careers or upgrading?
3. Are you thinking of returning to college for a degree?
4. Are you about to have a change in personal status: About to be married? About to be divorced? Are you widowed?
5. Are you permanently single (by choice)?
6. Are you likely to have a child in the next year or two?
7. Do you already have children?
8. Are you a single head of your household?
9. What are your sources of income? Salary? Dual income? Alimony? Investments? Other?
10. Are you now or are you about to become responsible for another person, such as a parent or spouse (returning to school or disabled)?
11. Are you nearing retirement age? How far ahead can you plan?
12. Do you have some major purchase (house, car, etc.) planned for the next year or two?
13. Do you plan to relocate in this country?
14. Do you want to live abroad?
15. How much time do you have available now for financial planning and education?

There are, of course, many questions that could be added to the list, but these will at least get you started and give you a basis from which to think and act. Often, some of these changes appear so obvious it just isn't apparent that they will cause substantial alterations in your financial life and profile. They all will, and they all must be allowed for and planned for. One of the primary purposes of goal-setting is to clarify your thinking, to force yourself to think through the situation in actuality, and then to project into the future and define how your goal can be accomplished and with what tools.

One interesting tool, the "blank check" technique, often used by employers of highly motivated sales people to help them stretch their thinking about how much they want to earn, may be useful to you. Simply take a blank check, make it out to yourself, and fill in the amount you want to earn this year or be worth in ten years.

This isn't as silly as it sounds. Writing out the check serves two purposes: It makes you think through precisely how much money you really want to have. Also, writing it down formally in this way constitutes a kind of mental commitment to the idea. It's an excellent personal motivator—if you don't make the check out for too little.

Next, try to relate your target to your own special skills or interests. At a recent financial mini-seminar conducted with six women, I asked them to write down their long-range goals. From the six, we selected Carla James's objectives to be reviewed by the group. Carla, the mother of three children, is nearing forty. She had two goals. The first was to put her three children through college; the second was to retire to a farm in her native Georgia.

After some discussion and figuring we determined that she would need roughly $150,000 over the next ten years. This figure is considerably less frightening when you break it down to $15,000 per year. Carla now had her financial goal. In other words, she had translated her goal into dollars. The next question was how to build that $150,000—which forced us all to get creative. We asked her question after question to get a profile of her capabilities and interests. She was working in the escrow department of a bank; before that she had been involved in real estate. Her response was quick. "Why don't I go into real estate, get my license? It seems so simple. Why didn't I see it before this?"

In fact, she did two things: She took *immediate* action; she signed up for a real estate license course that same day, and she also talked with several friends who were interested in finding the best possible real estate property investment in the area. She would do the research and legwork involved, she told them, in exchange for a percentage of the property. It took her six weekends, combing the real estate sections of the Sunday newspapers and marching through duplexes all over San Francisco, before she was ready to present two possible properties to her new partners. They selected one, and an attorney drew up a contract. Carla was given 10 percent of the property; in exchange for twelve days' intensive work she was a $7,000 partner in a real estate investment.

It all came about because she established a realizable financial goal, related it to her capabilities and enthusiasms, took immediate action, and kept her sights right on the target. As a happy postscript, she is now a successful real estate broker in San Francisco—and that initial investment sold several years ago for well over $100,000, raising her original $7,000 to over $10,000.

The final link to your goal-planning, then, is a relentless probe of your areas of interest and competence. The questions that follow are crucial, for they will help you establish your financial direction:

1. What are your interests and hobbies?
2. Do you have a flair for real estate, coins, furniture, stamps, art, flowers, cars, the stock market?
3. Are you creative? Can you write, paint, sculpt, build, whatever?
4. What areas of specialized knowledge do you have, however irrelevant they may seem at first?

If you don't seem to have any particular interests or strong suits, do some vocational shopping. Go to your local college and audit classes that cover various areas of investment, or join finance seminars. If one subject doesn't spark you, go on to the next. Your niche is there, but you must find it. And if this looks like a lot of legwork, it is. "No pains, no gains," as the old saying goes.

Above all, be venturesome. Rigidity is death to a creative money career approach. And don't be afraid to follow your "gut feeling." If the field in question is one you know something about, you'll find your instincts are generally reliable. Often enough the most modest opening can become your particular highway to financial self-realization.

In my own case, I'd been plodding along for a year as a secretary-researcher with Aerospace Components Corporation when I learned that my boss, contracts administrator for Aerospace, was leaving the company in a cutback. I managed to convince the brass that I had equipped myself to take over his job. What actually happened here was that management decided to save another expensive salary and give me the title and responsibility, but that was all right with me. I knew that to lift myself out of the ranks of the typewriter brigade, I had to first gain administrative experience and then maneuver myself into a position where my competence would be highly visible.

About the same time I took over as contracts administrator, Stanton acquired another small company (later to be called Infonics). It was so small, in fact, that it was operated in the same building with Aerospace, which allowed me to become involved in all its operations. I quickly became totally fascinated with the product line—tape duplicators—and I found myself being invited to sit in on meetings practically from day one. I learned everything about the product—purchasing, design, production, pricing and sales. In short, I was in the midst of a crash course in entrepreneurism, the chance of a lifetime for someone like me.

My own personal moment of truth came about a year later when Peter Stanton told me he had decided to sell Aerospace and devote all his time to the building of the new venture, Infonics, Inc. Would I be interested in coming along as sales manager and a corporate officer? I hesitated, but not for long. I had a natural flair for selling and I knew it. I'd found that out when I'd successfully handled the Infonics booth at a Los Angeles convention several months before. I knew the product inside and out, and I believed in it. I had developed complete confidence in Stanton's business acumen and drive. And I knew that I could best realize my own goals through participation in a fledgling company in a field with high growth potential.

It meant hard work and very long hours, as I knew it would. I had to organize a knowledgeable sales force from scratch, I had to go on the road myself to spread the tape-duplicating gospel at conventions and conferences of educators, industrialists, corporate management people—anyone and everyone who might provide a market for our product. I had to convince those hardheaded businessmen that audio-visual equipment had revolutionized education, which it certainly had, and that the world's best teachers could be brought into classrooms anywhere via the high-speed tape-duplicating equipment we were offering. I lived Infonics, waking and sleeping. I was on the road four months out of the year, setting up dealerships and making as certain as I could that only lively and capable people represented us.

And we brought it off. Two years later, while attending a trade fair, Peter Stanton and I were sipping brandy one night at the Principe e Savoia in Milan with our German distributor when we received a transatlantic call from George Otis, one of our associates. He announced that the Infonics stock had zoomed from $5 to $26 a share, or 200 times earnings; at that moment, one of us had become a millionaire and the other very comfortable . . . at least on paper. Unfortunately, I wasn't the millionaire, but I was hardly complaining! (What a feeling of celebration a moment like that brings: a sense of triumph that is unrivaled!) Eventually we sold Infonics to a larger, publicly traded corporation and again started a new venture.

That's how, in my early twenties, I skipped the long, weary climb through the executive echelons and vaulted at a bound into the ranks of management. I took a chance on a small outfit that presented a marvelous opportunity—as well as a few big ifs. True, we could have fallen on our faces, in which case I would have had to go back to square one. But my point here is that if you want to break out of the confines of the paycheck-every-Friday treadmill, you need to recognize your opportunity when it arises, and then have the courage to seize that chance and make the most of it. *Carpe diem.* Gather ye rosebuds. Oh, yes. Before it's too late.

The other side of that coin is illustrated by a woman who, thanks to her exceptional capabilities in organizing and running the internal affairs of my department, freed me to function in those areas for which I was best suited. On at least six separate occasions I brought up the possibility of her becoming a manager herself, but she always turned it down. And my offers were not the only ones she had. To this day I believe she could have been enormously successful in many areas of management, but she either would not or could not make that often frightening leap to freedom.

Perhaps, too, she was feeling not simply fear of failure, but that distinctly feminine malediction, fear of success. Sounds crazy, doesn't it? But listen to Matina Horner, president of Radcliffe College, who gave standard TAT achievement motivation tests to a sample of 90 females and 88 male students at the University of Michigan. She found that the brightest girls, odd as it may seem, were caught in a double bind that made them wary of reaching for their greatest potential.

"In testing and other achievement-oriented situations," Dr. Horner found, the brightest girl "worries not only about failure, but also about success. If she fails, she is not living up to her own standards of performance; if she succeeds, she is not living up to societal expectations about the female role. Men in our society do not experience this kind of ambivalence, because they are not only permitted but actively encouraged to do well."

Obviously a young woman conscious of what Dr. Horner calls the "psychological barrier" to feminine success isn't going to be very likely to set high goals for herself.

For a healthy antidote to this kind of diffidence I enthusiastically urge you to find yourself a role model, someone who has achieved to the full what you're seeking, or who stands for marked excellence in your field. Imitation isn't only the sincerest form of flattery, it builds incentive as well. And it's not just a spur, but an ego-builder too. You see that other women have left from humbler starting blocks than yours and have won their races. "She has done it," you can say to yourself at a particularly trying moment. "*I* can."

Of all the personal success stories I've known, the one that has most inspired me is that of Shirley R. Chilton, whom I've mentioned earlier. I first learned about her in a *Los Angeles Times* article, years before I made my own break for freedom. I was so impressed by her accomplishments that I wrote her and telephoned her once or twice, and although I didn't meet her until long after the Infonics venture had succeeded, she became for me the living example of what a woman can do when she is properly motivated and defines her goals—and, just as important, she disproves the tired old bromide that women involved in the financial world are "unfeminine." A vigorous, charming woman with curly red hair, Shirley Chilton is both a resounding business success and a devoted wife and mother.

The stepping stones of her career are a lesson in themselves. Upon U.S. entry into World War II, she served on the switchboard of the Bremerton Naval Station, handling top-secret traffic to the Pacific war fronts. Educated at the University of Washington as a sociologist, she was employed as a social worker by the state of California in San Diego, where, she says, she discovered that for her sociology was a dead end. "Only by upgrading the education of people can we improve their lot in life," she told me.

Mathematics had always fascinated her. "Through it I became interested in economics, and then in business and finance." Her education has been a continuing process. After special courses at Harvard, Columbia, and the University of Southern California and UCLA, she took her master's degree at Pepperdine and currently has her eye on a doctorate. Her avocation is still education, and she not only teaches at the present time but plans to increase her teaching load when she retires from business and write the children's books.

The jobs she held on her steady ascent to the financial heights suggest that unflagging energy with which she conquered a masculine province, always guided by her belief that "women are as knowledgeable as men *if* they are as dedicated to the field in which they operate." She was a flight crew instructor for United Air Lines, an accountant for the Packard Bell Company, secretary of a Seattle corporation; she then moved down to Los Angeles and joined Daniel Reeves and Company.

She continued her climb up the corporate ladder when she joined Hayden, Stone, Inc., where she served variously as operations manager, branch manager, regional manager, and finally vice-president—all the time continuing her education and, in 1967, embarking on a worldwide lecture tour with gold and the money markets as her topic. In 1969 she joined William O'Neil and Company, Inc., as assistant to the president.

In 1972, after Reeves's death, she held various positions from security analyst and portfolio adviser at Daniel Reeves and Company to president and chief executive officer—with nine *men* as the other partners who chose her for the number one spot. She is now chairman of the board.

I learned a great many things from studying Shirley Chilton's career. Here are a few of them:

1. Don't be satisfied with a title unless either more compensation or more responsibility goes with it. (In my own case with Aerospace I took the title because, despite the initially unsatisfactory salary, the authority to make some management decisions, and access to more knowledge about the product, came with it.)

2. Don't stay in a job that bores you, even if the salary is good. Ultimately it'll prove a dead end. You need to find satisfaction (genuine excitement, ideally) in the work you do if you're going to make a success of it.

3. Don't underrate yourself. (Plenty of other people will always be willing to do that job for you.) Having made yourself competent in your job, you should aim for the next rung up the company ladder, or for a position that promises fulfillment as well as opportunity. Always appraise your potential on the basis of the most rather than the least you can accomplish.

4. Don't fritter away time. This is a vital factor in achieving financial self-realization. If your job doesn't provide satisfaction, doesn't promise greater opportunity, doesn't pay well enough to allow you to make a start on your financial independence, you should waste no time in looking for a better one. Job-hopping is frowned on by many employers, of course, but remember—their concern is corporate, yours is personal. Preeminently successful women like Shirley Chilton haven't let mobility stand in their way. Neither should you. The possibility of a pension bestowed at the end of a long but unprofitable service to a company (unprofitable to *you*) should have no allure for you whatsoever.

Obviously a certain venturesome quality is necessary if you're going to make the most of the steadily increasing equality of opportunity in the business world. At some point or other you will have to take risks, trust your instincts. You cannot be turned aside by unfounded fears, or by people who do not share your vision of what you can accomplish. Confidence is the name of the game. And so is creative assertiveness. Analyzing your current situation, developing goals, deriving inspiration from role models, and enlarging your vision of what you can achieve will form the indispensable base for your program of financial freedom.

3 /

The Money Diet: You Can't Be Too Rich or Too Thin

Once you've decided to make money work for you, to use it as a tool in shaping and controlling your own destiny, you'll usually find that the first thing you need to do is straighten out your personal finances. You're probably in debt, right? I know debt is the American Way of Life, as they say, but it's not for you. You will have to get out of that hole before you can begin climbing toward your objective.

The money diet—moving yourself from the debit to the credit side of the ledger—is essential in achieving your long-range goal of financial liberation. It sounds simple: You stop spending and start saving. But, as most of us know from bitter experience, that isn't as easy as it sounds. It's much the same problem, in fact, that people confront when they want to stop putting on weight and begin losing it. The tough part is reversing the process. That's why I suggest a strict dieting regimen.

You won't win your financial independence until and unless you achieve a favorable credit position. People simply aren't going to trust you with money, the funds you may need to start your own business or initiate an investment plan or purchase real estate, until you've proved yourself responsible. And being in unpurposeful debt—*personal* debt—is not being responsible.

Like most women, I had virtually no training in how to

handle money. When I was in grade school my classmates and I were introduced to the school banking program, into whose tin coffers we were supposed to deposit twenty-five cents a week. And that was the beginning and the end of my formal financial education.

By the time I was fourteen and working part time, I found myself in a distressing credit situation. "Neither a borrower nor a lender be"? Fine, but I wasn't reading much Shakespeare. I *was* six months behind, on an average, in paying my debts. During my teens, having induced my parents to co-sign the applications, I'd acquired a number of charge accounts. I'd get my paycheck one day, and by the next day it had vanished into the waiting hands of my creditors. Sound familiar? The Great American Debt System was at work. If it works for everyone else, I thought, why shouldn't it work for me?

But of course it doesn't work for everyone else, either.

Naturally I felt terribly sophisticated and independent, being able to march into department stores and charge whatever caught my fancy. I simply had no sense of the reality of money. It was there, sometimes; that was all. I didn't realize how much of my income was being drained away by my having to pay the interest on revolving charge accounts for all the money I owed. I was on a treadmill that, for many Americans, keeps them jogging in one place for the rest of their lives. I was a financial disaster area before I was old enough to sign contracts legally.

By the time I'd turned twenty-three I was earning a salary of more than $20,000 a year and dealing with sizable financial matters on the corporate level. I was a "success"—but on the *personal* level the picture was different, and depressing. All that money coming in merely meant that I could have Lincolns instead of Mustangs, a larger and more elegant apartment, and designer clothes in my closets. It simply hadn't occurred to me that you must manage your own affairs as wisely as the management of a successful company manages *its* affairs.

The thought of putting part of my salary to work for me, of investing in something besides personal indulgence, hadn't entered my mind. The world of personal investments was a never-never land—single women just didn't go in for that sort of thing. It was part of what I call the Prince Charming Syndrome: You wait for Mr. Right to come along, sweep you off your feet, and take charge of your pampered future. A Robert Redford, say, with the business acumen of J. Paul Getty. . . .

It took me three years to come to my senses. At twenty-four I realized that liberation portended more than changing legalities; it threw open a world of unimagined possibilities. A woman could design and assume the responsibility for her own future. My identity was there for the taking. I began going out and seeking advice in the financial field, attending seminars for women in similar situations, and building up a small financial library. That step ultimately changed my world—because I am now in control of it.

Before that awakening (like many of you, I imagine), I tried various means of extricating myself from the quicksands of easy credit. One deceptively painless method is the debt consolidation plan: Typically, a bank or finance company asks you to bring in all of your bills and then makes a loan to you amounting to the total of all these bills plus a little extra for ready spending. With the loan you have received, you pay off all of your bills and are then left only with the loan payable to the finance company. Frequently the interest charged by the finance company exceeds the interest charged by your previous creditors. Equally important, the period of time over which the finance company loan is payable generally exceeds the average of the various bills it replaces. Since paying this stretched-out loan is relatively painless, you have a tendency to make new purchases and sink back into the morass of debt all over again.

That's what happened to me. Disregarding the warning of Bill Kuhns, a banker friend, I had my debts consolidated through a bank loan. It took me a short three months to get in trouble all over again. All this time the bank was collecting 12 percent on the money it had laid out for my creditors—just another bill added to *new* charges.

The fact, of course, is that there isn't any easy painless way of getting out of debt. *It is going to hurt.* You have to get out of your head the idea that you're standing under some gigantic, inexhaustible cornucopia. You must convince yourself that it really *isn't* un-American to jump off the perpetual getting/spending merry-go-round.

Your first goal is to get in control of your situation by pinning down specifically what it is that you have to tackle. (Which, as a fringe benefit, is also an excellent way of beating down panic.) There are two key steps here. The first is to determine your net worth today; the second is to anticipate your expenses and income for the next twelve months. These two documents are all that is required—but they are absolute musts.

Think of your Net Worth Calculation as a financial photograph of the dollar and cents side of you. We all have a net worth, but few of us know what it is. Your net worth can be negative as well as positive: That is, you may owe more than you own. If you *are* in trouble, the most important thing you can do is move right down the list to find out precisely how far in debt you are. Then and only then can you establish a plan of action.

Your Net Worth Calculation should be made at least once a year, unless you undergo some drastic change. Then you may have to do it more often. For it you will need to assemble various documents and do some research perhaps with your bank, employer, or stockbroker. The most important element is determining the current market value of things such as your house, car, jewelry, art, and other assets. Establishing current market value (what an item is worth *today*) can be done through various channels: Ads in your local newspaper, checking with your real estate broker or, for your car, checking the famous Blue Book.

What will all this tell you? How much you are worth, what

you own, what areas you are weak in. It will give you a financial photograph as well as a selling tool to use with your banker when applying for a loan.

The following form is simply a suggested outline; you will will undoubtedly have special additions or deletions to make. Your calculation should be done formally, preferably in ink. And I suggest that you keep it in a permanent folder, tagged "Jane Doe, Net Worth," or "Doe Family, Net Worth"—and be sure you date it. This is, by the way, the same type of calculation a company makes at least once a year. So you are, in effect, treating yourself like a corporation, as you should.

SUGGESTED NET WORTH CALCULATION

NET WORTH STATEMENT
OF

_____

DATE

Assets	*(Fill in amount)*
Cash on hand	$_____
Checking accounts	_____
Savings accounts	_____
Corporate profit-sharing plans— money now due you	_____
Marketable stocks (lower of cost or present market value)	_____
Money you have lent someone	_____
Life insurance (total cash surrender value)	_____
Bonds, including U.S. government	_____
Real estate	
Home (at market value)	_____
Investment properties	_____
Syndications	_____
Automobile(s), current market value	_____
Furs, jewelry, antiques, paintings (market value)	_____
TOTAL ASSETS	$_____

Liabilities   *(Fill in amount)*
Unpaid bills
  Charge accounts   _____
  Credit card accounts   _____
  Taxes (payable in next 12 months)   _____
  Insurance premiums
    (payable in next 12 months)   _____
  Rent (payable in next 12 months)   _____

Assets   *(Fill in amount)*
  Installment contracts   _____
  Loans: Banks
    Savings and loans   _____
    Insurance companies   _____
    Credit unions   _____
    Car loans   _____
  Mortgages
    House and other real property   _____

TOTAL LIABILITIES $_____

Summary of Net Worth Calculation

Assets $_____

Liabilities $_____

Net worth
  (assets minus liabilities) $_____

    Now that you've filled out your personal balance sheet, you know where you stand. Look hard at those two bottom lines. Do your liabilities exceed your assets? Then you are in trouble, and no two ways about it.

Debt is the slavery of the free, somebody said—some poor devil who undoubtedly went through it all. Once you've committed yourself to escape from the slavery of easy credit, you're ready for the money diet of programmed spending.

First take pencil and paper and make a list. The list, O Debtor, will be a careful breakdown—by analyzing each bill or obligation—of just how deep in debt you are. This has its painful side, I know. But you're going to face it now, resisting the temptation to shove that accusing column of figures in a drawer. The list is vital: It's not only proof that you're meeting your predicament head on; you'll also need it for your liquidation program.

Next, you work up an Accounts Payable Aging or Debt Aging. This has nothing to do with your going old and gray (at least, not directly). It's a common business term and it simply means determining how much you owe, and how old each of those outstanding bills is. They then need to be listed and dated according to whether they are 30, 60, or 90 days old. A typical accounts payable aging form looks like this:

DEBT AGING
(How Old)

Debt or Bill (example)	30 days	60 days	90 days	over 90
ABC Dept Store		$160.03		
Dr. Jones	$27.00			

Next, determine what portion of your income you can spare to pay off those bills on a monthly basis. That is the amount that needs to be divided into the total of all the bills outstanding. Here is where you must decide which bill cries out to be paid first. Here's one way of looking at it: If you have a credit card that is costing you 18 percent interest, you may be better off getting a loan from the bank at, say, 9 percent to 10 percent interest in order to pay it back. Yes, this is a form of debt consolidation, but when interest rates are extremely high it may make sense to go for that loan.

Now you're ready to take action. You must take command of the situation, having lost control of it by slipping into debt. Your first move is to quiet your creditors, not to avoid them or try to evade paying them—because an *eventual good credit rating will be crucial to your effort to make yourself financially independent.*

No matter how disgusted he may be with you, your creditor is likely to react with some sympathy if you offer your own, not a bank's or loan company's, debt consolidation plan. He values candor—possibly because he doesn't encounter it too often. *His* goal is to get paid, if not in 30 days, then eventually. If it takes you a year to pay off what you owe him, he's still in better shape than if he has to dip into his bad-debt reserve.

So write your creditors, frankly outlining your situation. Tell them exactly how you propose to go about paying, and the amount you will send them every week or month. The worst thing that can happen is that they'll turn your plan down—which, in the interests of eventual payment, they rarely do. A realistic plan is sure to meet with understanding. The letter should be sent to *all* your creditors, including department stores—even though this move is quite likely to result in the temporary suspension of your charge privileges (which may, in turn, be a blessing in disguise).

You must remember that this program will work only once. After those envelopes drop through the slot, you're committed. You cannot expect your creditors, who have agreed to your proposal, to be as amiable if you send out a second series of letters begging off. The essential point is to propose a payoff rate that won't cripple you, and then *stick to the program*, no matter how much it hurts.

Once you've reached an agreement with your creditors, you should take a long, hard look at your fixed expenses and eliminate all purchasing that isn't strictly necessary. And this means—you guessed it, fellow sufferer—budgeting: or what I prefer to call a money plan.

There are no two ways about it: Putting together a money plan is an out-and-out headache, which is why so few people ever do it. My first budgeting trial-by-fire began with my early corporate experience. Every quarter it was part of my job to submit a budget for my department for the forthcoming year. My budget requirements (the money my section needed) were then combined with the other departments' requirements so that top management could compute an overall budget. Then the fun began—the rigorous chopping of outlay demanded by management.

I had to forecast what I was going to spend on advertising, sales promotion, flight transportation, hotels, conventions, and printing of brochures, as well as the salaries and commissions for the people in my department—all of which was, of course, to be subtracted from my sales forecast figures. Frankly, I hated every minute of it.

But it's absolutely essential—for people, not just for companies. How else can the money people know how much they need to support your plans, or what is required overall? And, almost as important, what simply can't be allowed? Maybe it all boils down to the fact that, in life as in business, there simply is no room for surprises that could have been anticipated. God knows, there are enough surprises that *can't* be planned for.

In the case of my private finances, after being clobbered with some unpleasant surprises—taxes, a big insurance premium, or some other out-of-the-blue bill—I began to realize that I could have planned for that "surprise" months in advance, which would have made its arrival a lot less painful. Its size would have been reduced by prorating (and saving) the sum over those intervening months.

Take it from me, a money plan is vital to your financial liberation, and you might as well get started on it. Now.

It's part of the involvement process, too. The further you get involved—the more *un*pleasant it becomes and the more rules you follow—the sooner you can begin feeling better about your financial situation. It's like skiing. Those downhill racers look as though they're just wishing their way down the mountain, swooping and gliding along, yet behind that seemingly effortless grace lie thousands of hours of hard, even painful practice and a grueling training regimen.

Some good news: For a money plan there are actually only two categories with which you need concern yourself. The first is your *income*, which should include salary and any other income you receive on a regular or periodic basis (stock dividends, alimony, annuity payments, and so on). Second is *outflow*, which includes fixed expenses such as rent or mortgage payments, utilities (heating, fuel, electricity, telephone, gas, water), insurance, loan payments, charge accounts, clothing, food, and so on. Plus *savings*. Yes. Place that in your outflow category, too, in order to ensure that you *do* set those amounts aside, regularly.

Now for those big bills that come like thunderbolts here and there during the year, such as taxes, insurance premiums, school tuition, and vacations. They should be spread over a monthly pattern rather than absorbed in one indigestible chunk in the week they occur. Let's take taxes as an example. Both income and property taxes can be estimated well in advance, either by referring to your last year's assessments or by getting the applicable tax tables from an accountant. All you need to do then is take that lump sum and divide it by twelve. For example, $1,560 divided by 12 = $130 a month. (Which looks a lot less frightening.) You then place that amount in each column-month. It should be kept in a checking or savings account.

What you're doing here is evening out the bumps (and shocks) by dealing with them on a monthly basis. A hundred dollars for an insurance premium twice a year may sting, but $16.60 per month is a breeze.

And if you're worrying about where to get the figures for all of this, don't. You probably have all the information you need right there in your checkbook—rent or mortgage payments, department store bills, grocery checks, and so on. All you have to do is break them down into their various categories from the past year, tally them up, and you're off and running. By the way, your first effort at budgeting will probably be the most difficult; each year the process becomes easier and less time-consuming.

Now check your totals. Are you even? Or does your outflow exceed your income? If you're ahead, you may use that surplus as you see fit. If you're behind, you must cut back ruthlessly wherever you can. But don't simply tighten your belt. Get creative about your situation: Look around you, explore your possibilities, search for "hidden" money.

Look for things that can be converted into cash, such as old sports equipment, a painting you're tired of, furniture you no longer use, whatever. You might want to consider getting an extra job, or going after a raise in your current position. Also, call in any loans possible that you may have made to friends or relatives.

To get yourself on the right fork in the road toward independence from money worries, you should take 10 percent off the top and put it in a savings account, no matter what. That is going to make for still more belt-tightening at a time when you're also paying off your debts; but it is essential, not only as self-discipline but as a cushion against the unexpected.

Before placing your money in a savings account, it's wise to shop around. The competition among banks and savings and loan companies is so fierce that you should take advantage of it. Obtain the highest rate of interest possible. Read pertinent articles in *Consumer's Report*.

When determining which savings bank to use, you should be aware that the rates are constantly changing and will also vary from bank to bank. As you probably know, there are many different types of accounts, each of them carrying with it a set of government-established penalties that apply should you withdraw your funds prior to maturity. Generally, the shorter the period of time you are willing to keep your money "locked up," the lower the rate of interest you'll enjoy.

You can tell a lot about savings banks by the way the people there respond to your questions about interest, penalties, and so on. If they're hesitant or seem less than straightforward, it's a good idea to cross them off your list. Always remember: Where savings are concerned, *you* are in a buyer's market. That may be your only leverage. Use it wisely.

When shopping for bank accounts, you should ask the following questions (where applicable):

1. Cost per check on various kinds of accounts?
2. Monthly cost, if any?
3. Minimum balance and charge for dropping below minimum?
4. Free checking accounts available?
5. Overdraw account available to new customers? If so, at what rates of interest?
6. Cost for printed (personalized) checks in quantities of 250 or 500?
7. Other costs?
8. Bounced-check charge (overdraft)?
9. Stop payment?
10. Traveler's checks?
11. Safe deposit box?
12. Cashier's checks?
13. Certified checks?
14. Notary service?

Unless you're unemployed or cliff-hanging on the brink of total insolvency, you should be able to pay off your obligations within nine months. The first ninety days are the hardest, just as they are in sloughing excess fat from your body, but after that rather grim initial period you'll find there's a certain joy attached to self-discipline. Now you're down to muscle. And all the while you're ridding yourself of constant worry over bills and payments, you're also lightening your spirits with the fact that your bank account is steadily growing.

Your program of debt relief to enhance your financial picture will require certain tools, as does the Weight

Watchers' dieting plan. One requirement for Weight Watchers is an accurate food-weighing scale; merely eye-balling a serving of food and guessing at the calorie count is not likely to result in much improvement in your figure.

For debt watchers a similar system is essential. Part of your trouble in the past was your habit of stuffing bills and other papers into drawers all over the place—out of sight, out of mind. (I know: It takes a thief to catch a thief.) Whatever paper work you had to do probably was performed in haste and impatience on a corner of the dining-room table or in the chaos of the phone stand.

Instead of that helter-skelter game you've been playing for so long, adopt a businesslike procedure. Set aside an alcove, a small room, or at least the corner of a room for handling your financial affairs. Make that financial corner as attractive as possible, and make sure you have a clear surface for working. Equip your corner with a good lamp, two file folders for paid and unpaid bills, another file for canceled checks, and manila folders for other documents and papers such as records of time payments on a car or appliances, receipts for tax-deductible items, stock transactions, W-2 forms, insurance forms. It's also important to select a certain day for meeting your monthly obligations. Most billings are sent out around the twenty-fifth; I've found it's a good idea to set aside a particular, regular day between the first and tenth of the succeeding month to make out checks and mail them off.

A friend of mine, who used these very steps to climb out of debt, has equipped a room in her house like a small office, complete with desk, four-drawer filing cabinet, fresh flowers to cheer her flagging will, and her indispensable $19.95 electronic calculator. She refers to it as "the room"—and she now runs her successful real estate ventures and other investments from it. She has also collected and developed a fairly comprehensive investment library, which is housed there.

I want to say a few words about my friend's electronic calculator: It's probably the most important gadget you can own. It not only makes the bill-paying and checkbook-balancing easier (and more accurate!), but it can give you an increased confidence and facility over money management. You can buy such calculators for less than twenty dollars. And the calculator has other uses, too. Slip it into your handbag when you go shopping, even at the grocery store, and total up your bill as you buy each item. There's no easier way to compute the price per measure (the cost of an item per weight or ounce) and to determine your savings on larger purchases. By the way, if you use a calculator for your taxes or in your business, that percentage of its use may be tax-deductible.

A successful and effective life is the result of productive habits made second nature; perhaps the most necessary habit to encourage is constant *awareness* of outflow as well as income. Obviously your financial base will not be broadened unless you can consciously hold the outflow down as much as possible, especially during periods of inflation. The *habit* of comparative pricing will take you much farther than blindly scrimping, reducing yourself to a bare subsistence level.

The success of your personal economy will depend on the intelligence with which you buy the things you need. You must learn to think of yourself as a company's purchasing agent, charged with keeping the cost of everything from office supplies to the output of the coffee machine as low as possible.

That's why I suggest that you add one more item to your financial corner: a little notebook, to be carried in your purse, in which you'll keep records of your purchases and comparative prices. Consulting it during one of those nonsale sales at a dress shop not only will act as a brake to an impulse purchase, but will sharpen your eye for comparative prices. From my own experience I know that 98 percent of the things you buy can be bought elsewhere at a discount.

Deficit spending in the personal as well as the governmental sphere has become very fashionable in the last quarter century. But there is more than one sign pointing to a 180-degree turnabout in these times. In any case, you'll find that it's a lot more comforting to keep the bills down, pay them on the dot, and gain enough liquidity (gained partly through *not* paying that murderous 18 percent interest on your purchases) to embark on a solid money program.

All right. You've gone, say, nine months on the money diet, and you've settled a lot of things. You've proved yourself responsible, your saving habit has now become ingrained, and you know that an unforeseen doctor's bill won't throw your new life style out of gear. You shouldn't need a crash diet again. Now it's a question of holding the line and keeping in shape. You understand the bone and sinew of your own financial structure. You're ready to step out now with brand-new confidence. You're ready to establish a sound credit position and begin evaluating the various elements of your financial foundation including savings, real estate, stocks and much more. You're ready to be creative instead of negative. You're ready to talk to your local banker.

4

Women and Credit

"Women," it has been said, "don't get the credit they deserve—in more ways than one." It's no secret that until very recently women were automatically second-class citizens when it came to general credit cards and, most importantly, loan and mortgage applications. Department stores and consumer-goods manufacturers sought to win our business by granting credit, it's true; but in the more important, long-term credit areas, such as buying a house, we were still looked upon as flighty if not downright unsound—"below men and above children," as Lord Chesterfield put it so quaintly.

All that is changing rapidly under pressure from women's groups and state and federal laws that forbid credit discrimination. When the First Los Angeles Bank announced a few years ago that it would count alimony payments and investments as income when deciding whether or not a female applicant was worthy of credit, a milestone was passed.

First Los Angeles is, in fact, in the vanguard of the movement to break down credit barriers to women. The Citizens Savings and Loan Association, California's fourth largest, is going after the growing market among single women for the less expensive town houses and condominiums. Perhaps even more dedicated to the proposition that women should have equal access to credit is New York's First Women's Bank and Trust Company. Madeline McWhinney, a former economist for the Federal Reserve Bank, is its president, and Betty Friedan, Pauline Trigere, Jane Trahey, and Eileen Ford are among its directors.

"We will certainly not discriminate against men," President McWhinney has stated, but obviously her institution will be oriented toward women's financial needs.

Before the welcome changes in bankers' and credit companies' philosophy, horror stories abounded about the difficulties women, no matter how capable or responsible they were, experienced in obtaining credit, especially long-term credit. And plenty, alas, still abound. Representative Leonor K. Sullivan of Missouri recently conducted congressional hearings on that subject. A parade of witnesses testified that when a married woman regains single status, through divorce or widowhood, her credit cards are often automatically canceled because they were in her husband's name. "When a man dies, everything stops. When a woman dies, nothing stops."

Congressional investigation also disclosed that when a young woman with a good credit rating marries she may often find her credit status downgraded if her husband is a student or a serviceman with a minimal income. Representative Edward I. Koch quoted a letter from one such woman: "While living in New Jersey, we tried to get a charge account at a discount chain. The credit department admitted they had turned us down because his rank as a serviceman was too low, although had I been single my job would have been enough to get me an account."

Banking and other credit institutions have made it a practice to discount all or part of a working wife's salary when it is noted on a mortgage application; if she is of childbearing age, it is assumed that she will soon leave the work force. For years, single women have found it next to impossible to obtain a mortgage, and as for a woman securing a loan to start her own business—forget it!

One incident that turned many institutions around—as an executive of Citizen's Savings and Loan frankly admitted —was an action taken by Christine and Richard Carroll, a Brooklyn couple in their thirties. The Carrolls brought suit against two savings and loan companies, charging sex discrimination, after the couple was denied a mortgage on the grounds that his $12,500 annual income was insufficient to guarantee repayment. Mrs. Carroll's $4,000 annual salary was not counted at all, although they have only one daughter and explained that they did not plan to have any more children. Following a great deal of publicity, the suit was dropped. One of the savings and loan companies offered the Carrolls a mortgage.

Another pressure point in the controversy over credit discrimination against women has been the national credit-card business. A number of women earning more than $10,000 a year complained that their applications had been rejected, without explanation, by Diners' Club, American Express, or BankAmericard. Responding on its own, National Bank-Americard, Inc., issued a strongly worded advisory to its 250 member banks to furnish credit cards solely on the basis of willingness and ability to pay, without regard to the sex of the applicant. Other companies have also been falling into line —not, let it be said, without a good deal of strife that has surfaced in testimony before various legislative, congressional, and federal commission hearings.

Mayor Kathryn Kirschbaum of Davenport, Iowa, was deemed competent to govern that city of 103,000 souls. Yet she was denied a BankAmericard because her husband hadn't signed the application! Mayor Kirschbaum took her case to the Iowa Civil Rights Commission and won the right to have a credit card of her own.

And there was the case of Sheila Widnall, an associate professor of aeronautical engineering at the Massachusetts Institute of Technology, who was informed that she must obtain her husband's signature before she could get a loan from M.I.T.'s federally chartered credit union. The grounds for denying her a loan without her husband's cosignature were simple: She "might get pregnant and leave the faculty." Professor Widnall got her loan only after active intervention by the institute's administration.

The debt we owe these and other women is huge; their

efforts are resulting in long overdue changes. Twenty-two states and the District of Columbia have passed antidiscriminatory laws affecting women's credit, with more to follow. And now the federal Equal Credit Opportunity Act outlaws sexual discrimination in commercial and consumer credit. A new amendment has been attached to the Small Business Administration Act preventing this agency, for the first time, from discrimination against female applicants for business loans.

All well and good. But how will *you* handle your own credit opportunities? How can you take advantage of the new credit breakthroughs open to you? "If you would know the value of money, go and try to borrow some." How true, Poor Richard!

First of all, keep in mind that there are two kinds of credit. One is constructive, the other destructive. *Constructive* credit (indebtedness) is the amount you may owe on, say, a real estate investment, or on stock investments purchased on margin. This use of indebtedness is creative—it's a kind of financial leverage you must exert in order to succeed.

An example of *destructive* credit would be the irresponsible use of credit cards when you don't have the money to back up the spending. A good rule to follow here is that a credit card—and I speak from sad experience—should *never* be used unless you already have the money in the bank or can clearly identify where the money will come from, and when. I'll have more to say about credit cards a bit farther on. For now let's content ourselves with the obvious and hard truth that a credit card is a money tool, *not* a supplement to money. The failure to make this distinction has "supplemented" many a poor soul right into bankruptcy.

Assuming your sights are firmly set on constructive credit, there are several areas you should explore immediately. Again, do your homework. Get out your pad and pencils and make a list, ticking off the items as you've checked them out:

1. Make a careful and precise inventory of your assets.

Include your current bank balance, savings account, real estate holdings, life insurance policies, stock certificates, automobile, jewelry, and so on. I know you've already done this when you worked out your Net Worth Calculation; but, like a will, this kind of personal accounting is valuable only if it's kept right up to date. And there are other reasons. Making a detailed inventory is not only good for the morale (almost invariably you find you're better off than you thought you were); it will also enable you to supply quick, accurate answers when you're interviewing the credit people.

2. Know your rights. In October 1974 President Ford signed the Equal Credit Opportunity Act. It is the first across-the-board federal law designed to protect women's credit rights. To quote its first paragraph: "It shall be unlawful for any creditor to discriminate against any applicant on the basis of sex or marital status *with respect to any aspect of a credit transaction.*" (The italics are mine, but the franchise is yours.)

This law has teeth: Any woman victimized by such discrimination may *(a)* bring action to "recover actual damages and five hundred dollars ($500) in addition thereto, for each willful violation," and *(b)* "petition the court to order the person violating the Law to extend credit upon such terms, conditions and standards as he normally utilizes in granting credit to males."

Find out, too, just how far your particular state has advanced in eliminating sex discrimination in the credit field. You can obtain copies of the new laws affecting women's credit from your county clerk's office or, failing that, from the clerk of your state legislature. For example, the California Civil Code is very, very explicit about the granting of credit to women, echoing the national Equal Credit Opportunity Act almost to the letter. Some say it doesn't go far enough—that there is a potential escape hatch in what's called the "relevant factor" clause, which might allow creditors to refuse credit to a working woman who becomes pregnant. It's a question that will no doubt have to be tested in the courts. My point here is that you are an American citizen endowed with equal rights. It's up to you to avail yourself of them.

3. Make a slow, careful survey of your local banks. This is vital. *Bankers are the center of your financial universe*. That's a very strong statement, so let me give you a few examples of just how important they can be. Not only do they offer many services in addition to checking and savings accounts, from loans to escrow departments to trust departments, but should you decide to buy a house or invest in real estate, it is your banker who will review your loan application. He also has the power to influence the loan committee. He may even be a member of it, which makes a difference, of course, when it comes to personal loans as well.

An aside here—an unnecessary one, I hope. The most basic point in applying for credit is the fact that you must have a bank account, *in your own name*, in order to establish personal credit. This may sound absurdly elementary, but I only recently learned that one of my close friends, a Vassar honors graduate with a top teaching position, has for the first time in her thirty-seven years opened a bank account. She had grown up in a conservative small town whose citizens all knew one another and where all transactions were handled on a cash basis. That simple, gracious way of life simply isn't relevant in today's mobile, credit society.

And the account, I repeat, should be *in your own name*. This is one area that even today is often overlooked, particularly by married women. Under the new credit laws this situation will change in the near future; nonetheless, it is important for you to assure yourself of a sound credit position should you become widowed, divorced, or separated. As matters stand at the moment, if a man dies everything stops. Why? Because the credit in three out of four cases is in *his* name. Therefore, what every women should do in establishing her own credit is to create small checking and savings accounts—say, a few hundred dollars each—and perhaps buy her next television set, dishwasher, or car on an installment loan through her bank.

It's a matter of personal policy. Even if you're capable of paying cash for these items, buying them on credit affords you the opportunity to establish credit-worthiness under your own name, for a small fee. After you've paid off this small installment loan, you can then progress to having all credit cards in both your names, by which time you'll be launched on your own individual credit development program. This is not to say that credit in a marriage should not be worked out between the two of you. It should, but the bottom line to the contract at the moment is that when you work together under the existing credit laws in most states you are setting up *his* credit, not yours.

Single or married, credit cards can be a one-way express ticket to disaster, or steady proof of your competence and integrity as a debtor. It's up to you. Along with bank loans, they comprise the quickest and easiest way of establishing yourself as a worthwhile credit risk. Without some sort of reading on your ability and willingness to pay your debts, a prospective creditor has no way of telling whether or not you can be trusted. There's the classic story of the millionaire who applied for a credit card and was turned down because he'd never borrowed money or charged anything. Maybe the system *is* wrong, essentially, but you're not (presumably) a millionaire, and that *is* how the game is played.

Granting the importance of credit cards in establishing your credit-worthiness, what sort are most useful to you, and in what order? Assuming you've gone on the money diet and completed the repayment of an installment loan, the credit cards you may want to apply for are, in order of priority: (1) gasoline credit cards, (2) department store credit cards, and (3) general credit cards such as Master Charge, BankAmericard, and American Express.

You should realize that during the first several months (at which time you may be given a very low limit on your account, $300 or so), the credit card companies will be watching that account very carefully in order to determine whether or not you are "credit-worthy." If you prove yourself to be so, your card is likely to be reissued for an extended period of time and a higher credit limit. Therefore it is crucial that you are meticulous in meeting the terms of the contract, never stretching out your payments (and paying that 18 percent interest) or accidentally exceeding your credit limit.

If you've been turned down for a loan or a credit card, be sure to find out, immediately, why, and what credit reporting service was used. Under the current Fair Credit Reporting Act of 1971, the company supplying the information that leads to a rejection of credit must furnish without charge the nature and substance of the information on file with that agency. After you receive a copy, you can evaluate why you were rejected, and take advantage of an opportunity to rectify any incorrect information.

Also, if you're just plain curious about your credit rating or what's in your credit file, that information is available to you for a negligible fee. One firm that functions on a nationwide basis is TRW Credit Data, which more than likely has a credit file on you. They have offices across the United States. If you're interested in more information on the Fair Credit Reporting Act or other matters relating to credit, address your inquiries to your local TRW Credit Data office or any of the other credit reporting agencies in your area.

A lesson I've learned over the years in filling out credit references is to avoid filling them out at the bank or credit institution. Take them home or to your office for completion, and *always* make a photostat of credit applications (as well as any other forms you may fill out).

The main thing is to think of credit as a tool—in many ways the most important one you'll have to work with. Used intelligently and constructively, it will help you build your future. Credit cards are an important part of this; long-term credit *follows* the establishment of credit-worthiness and is, of course, far more important.

Which gets us back to banks and bankers—the name of the game. In granting you credit, institutions will be looking for what the venerable publication *The Banker's Handbook* refers to as "the three C's of credit—character, capital, and capacity—which simply means '*Does* the person pay? *Can* the person pay? *Will* the person pay?'"

Some of your qualifications for credit-worthiness will be your length of residence, your checking and savings accounts records, employment information (how long you've held your job, your position, your income), as well as your previous credit history, current indebtedness, and collateral (home-ownership, stocks, bonds, treasury bills, or T-bills, insurance policies, and so on).

In fact, in rating these various factors, lending institutions commonly use the following type of credit-scoring point system. You might want to go through it and total up your score to determine your particular credit-worthiness. (A word of caution: This credit scoring was developed almost exclusively for installment loans; it is not necessarily used by every bank or lending institution across the board.)

Marital status: Married, add one point.

Dependents: One to three, add two points; four or more, add one point.

Age.: 21–25, add one point; 26–64, add two points; over 65, add one point.

Residence: Over five years at same address, add one point.

Previous residence: Over five years at previous address, add one point.

Job status: Less than one year at present job, add no points; one to three years, add one point; four to six years, add two points; seven to ten years, add three points; over ten years, add four points.

Monthly obligations: Less than $200, add one point; over $200, add no points.

Type of work: If you are in one of the professions, an executive or foreman, add three points; skilled worker, add two points; blue-collar worker, add one point; anything else, add no points.

Loans: If you have a loan at the bank where you are applying for credit, add five points; if you have loan experience at another bank or finance company, add three points.

Bank accounts: If you have a checking or savings account at the bank where you are applying for credit, add two points.

Telephone: Listed in your name, add two points.

Now add up your points. If you have eleven or more, you are likely to be considered a good credit risk.

What you should keep uppermost in your mind is that once you enter the financial world you'll find that everything you do is linked to your banking activities. If you are starting a company or any financial venture of your own, your banker will serve as a character reference to your potential associates or investors. If you open an account at a stockbrokerage, you will be asked by your broker who your banking references are, and your banker will then be called upon to verify the amount of money you have in your account and to give a character reference. All of which means that developing a close and understanding relationship with your banker has to be one of of your most valuable financial assets.

This does *not* mean that you should approach your banker with fear and trepidation. I know that most of us are or have been rather timid about approaching banks. There's a somber, forbidding atmosphere that often surrounds money in an institutional setting. A lot of this is a legacy of the past fifty years, when banks were deliberately built to look like money temples, their high-vaulted ceilings echoing and re-echoing like the nave in Westminster Abbey. Then there are those heart-rending movies of the thirties on the Late Show, with the impoverished farmer sitting hangdog with his hands between his knees, at the mercy of the well-fed, well-dressed banker behind the big mahogany desk. . . .

Well, architecture has changed since World War I, and so have attitudes. A banker is a man who lends you an umbrella when the weather is fair, the saying went, and takes it away from you when it rains. Not true—not now. Banks don't make money by turning down loan applications, and credit companies can't make money on you until they issue you a credit card. Unfortunately, all too many women have the relationship reversed: We feel that credit and lending institutions are doing us a favor, instead of realizing that we are the customers—that we are doing *them* a favor in bringing them our business. They may not look like it, but bankers are really salemen selling a commodity. That commodity simply happens to be money.

This is a crucial point to bear in mind. It's also important that you sit down and discuss, obviously on a confidential basis, your future plans. Whether you're interested in starting a small company, opening trust accounts for your children, or looking into real estate possibilities, your banker can be very helpful indeed. He talks with other members of the business and financial community. It's his business to know what's going on. He may be able to tell you about some new development within the community that you may want to take advantage of. He can be a good source of reference for a reputable stockbroker or tax attorney (he deals with them continually), or for a good corporate or general attorney. He's also a key reference if you're renting an apartment or applying for a job.

So much for his importance and your basic approach. Now let's get down to tactics.

When you open an account you should select an important branch of the bank, one whose manager will have enough influence to sway the loan committee. If possible, deal with the main branch of the institution. If it is not practical for you to deal with the main office, pick an office in a wealthy part of town where the depositors are likely to be people of substance. This sort of branch will typically be managed by an up-and-coming bank executive with some clout within his own institution. Find out the name and title of the manager from the switchboard operator or from the manager's secretary. In most cases, his title would be vice-president. Introduce yourself to the manager no matter how unapproachable he may seem, remembering that it's his job to foster good relations with potential customers. A telephone call to make an appointment is all that's usually needed. Decide beforehand what you plan to say, even if it's all futures. Make a list (homework again), reduce it to five or six key phrases, jot them down on a three-by-five card in the order you'd like to present them, and commit them to memory. (You'd be surprised how many people in the highest circles of government and finance do this before an important meeting.)

State your case simply and concisely, remembering that the manager's time is valuable, as is yours. You might start out by telling him that you need a loan of, say, $2,800, repayable over 24 months. Briefly describe what you need the money for, tell him what you do for a living—how much money you make, and how much you can set aside for the repayment of the loan (don't forget to include interest)—and hand him a personal balance sheet, already filled out. He will no doubt ask you to recopy the balance sheet onto the bank's form and sign it, but he will be impressed by the fact that you have made one up in advance. You can probably clinch the good impression you have created by summarizing your credit record. (Tell him that you previously borrowed from X Bank and paid the loan back promptly, and that you have a fine credit record at the ABC Department Store.)

It's often a good idea to select the bank with which your employer does business. Whatever your position with the firm, you're likely to get special treatment at the bank because, in many instances, they quite naturally assume that you may have some influence over your employer's banking interests. It's a perfectly legitimate form of leverage. Use it.

Even if you work in a very large corporation, it is amazing how much preferential treatment you are likely to get if you use your employer's bank, particularly if you use the particular branch at which your employer does a great deal of business. Don't forget, of course, to inform whomever you deal with that you work for the client company.

When I say "cultivate a warm and open relationship with your banker" I don't mean the pleasant young man at the third teller's window, helpful though he may have been to you. You must seek out an official—a vice-president at least, and best of all the vice-president in charge of loans. As you may know, banks have a great many officers. Normally, each branch will have at least two or three, and sometimes quite a few more. Bank officers range from assistant cashiers to the chairman of the board. In a typical branch, you may encounter an assistant cashier, a cashier, an assistant vice-president, and a vice-president (usually the branch manager). A large bank may have dozens of vice-presidents; they are the ranking officers below an executive vice-president, and, usually, the highest-level officer found in a branch.

Again—I cannot stress this too much—a supplicatory attitude is not going to impress a bank manager with large sums of money at his disposal. It is your self-assurance, your clear-headedness, your drive that will produce results.

In countless cases, bankers extend loans with no collateral at all, simply on the basis of their confidence in the client's ability to repay the loan. A Boston sales executive with thirty years' experience in the mutual fund field found himself faced with a severe personal crisis and approached a vice-president of one of the city's most venerable banking houses for a $10,000 loan. When the officer asked him what he could offer as collateral, the executive looked him right in the eye and answered: "My good name on the Street." He got the loan.

I remember one woman who described to me a potentially desperate financial crisis. She needed to buy a house; she also knew the bank would never grant her a mortgage, given her current resources. She did not have a salaried job, and was just starting out in real estate, on commission. What did she do? She telephoned the president of her bank for an appointment, went in, and forcefully presented her case. The banker was so impressed with her professionalism, her obvious strength of character and force of will, that he approved the loan himself, bypassing the loan committee. She is today one of Southern California's most successful real estate brokers and works regularly with this same banker. Boldness, a quiet self-assertion can pay off. One reason (sometimes hard to believe, but true) is that bankers are people, too.

This is still another reason for dealing with the top echelons, wherever you go. In most banks, the vice-president in charge of loans has access to a discretionary fund of, say, $50,000 to $100,000, and is empowered to grant loans up to that amount *on his own signature*. That pleasant young man at the teller's window couldn't approve a $500 loan if his life depended on it. So go where decision-making and risk-taking are a way of life—at the top.

5 /

Choosing the Pros

The problem of selecting and working with professionals has always intrigued me—there's such an atmosphere of apprehension and intimidation that always seems to surround the process. Early on in my career people were always talking about contacting their brokers, or waiting to "get in touch with" their lawyers. Everyone seemed to have a smoothly functioning team of professionals he or she could summon forth like that wonderfully helpful djinn in the *Arabian Nights*, simply by picking up a phone. I guess I assumed they were just around—until I needed to get a car loan. Then all at once I realized that while people are always talking about accountants, legal specialists, and brokers, no one ever tells you how to go about getting one.

The plain fact of the matter was I didn't know where to look, or what to do after I got there. Like so many women (and, be it added, so many men), I'd felt that sense of intimidation that clouds our dealings with all professionals: the batteries of proprietary secretaries and assistants, the marble-walled offices, the huge desks and elegant appointments. And also that clutch of self-deprecation—"How can I possibly justify taking this important person's time?" As a friend of mine said, recounting a frustrating interview with an attorney: "He was a lawyer, right? Which automatically meant that he was smart and I was dumb."

That kind of thing. Well, I've emerged from this particular personal tunnel (not without a few scars) with a few points to pass along. The sense of intimidation, I think, stems from the fact that you know you need help, but you don't know how it is they're going to help you. They know something (a lot of things, in fact) you don't, which you *think* puts you at a disadvantage.

But try looking at it this way: Instead of furniture or cars or clothing, a professional has special knowledge for sale, and you are deciding whether you'll hire that knowledge or not. Watch your big executives: They have no qualms whatever about going out and finding themselves the best CPA or stockbroker they can.

You've encountered the problems in choosing professionals yourself, in areas far removed from finance. Take, for instance, the woman who wanders into a beauty salon, lets herself be thrown by the *haut décor* and intimidated by "Mr. George," and emerges with the sort of coiffure that suits her only by the wildest stroke of luck. If, on the other hand, she does some careful research, selects a really top-notch stylist, explains clearly and concisely what she wants or doesn't want, and then listens to (and coolly evaluates) what Mr. George has to tell her, she stands an excellent chance of getting the hair style that will suit her and captivate others.

All right, then. Hair is hair, and it grows back even if it's butchered. Money—*your* money—is too painfully come by for you to be careless about the protection you're seeking for it. The name of the game is getting the very best talent you can; and here, reputation is of crucial importance. You wouldn't think of buying a stock with a poor reputation; the same holds true for the professionals.

I've already stressed the tremendous importance of your bankers in your campaign for financial self-realization (and no one *is* more vital to you), and further on I'll deal with the selection of a stockbroker. Right now I want to talk about the pattern of expertise you will need in order to achieve your financial self-realization.

In my own financial affairs, which include both business and personal needs, I've retained what I refer to as my basic six—the pros I work with on a continual basis (I've listed them roughly in order of importance):

Banker
Lawyer
Stockbroker
CPA/tax accountant
Real estate broker
Insurance agent

You should make up your own list. You may have a need for highly specialized talents such as those furnished by an art or antiques appraiser, a business manager or patent attorney. If you do, add them to the above.

So how *do* you select those top-flight professionals you can work with closely and effectively toward achieving your goals? Over the years I've put together a simple step-by-step check list I've found to be consistently successful in choosing *all* professionals, both in and outside of the financial community. Here it is:

1. *Define your need.* This sounds silly, but invariably you'll find it helps in clarifying and focusing your problem. Perhaps the greatest area for error lies in asking the wrong pro about the wrong thing. Take lawyers, who many people think are automatically financial wizards. Most of them are not. Patent law and criminal law, for instance, are like apples and bananas and have no tie-in with finance. I remember a friend talking about a real estate negotiation and saying of her legal counsel, "But he was only a corporate lawyer, he didn't know enough about real estate to be very helpful." In other words, he should have been a real estate lawyer. Today there are specialists within the specialty. We live in a diversified, highly technical world. Recognize that.

The single exception here is, of course, the attorney who specializes in areas of the financial field such as taxation or estate planning. By defining your need you may also find you can get your answer or have your matter handled *without fee* by your banker, say, or by your employer or even yourself (with a little vigorous research at the local library)—in which case you'll save yourself some money. You also should determine how long you'll be needing these services, whether on a one-shot or an ongoing basis.

2. *Make a list of three.* Once you've ascertained that you require, for example, an attorney, get the names of three—not less, and probably not more (I've found that more than three involves too much time and effort). Here are ways to find that list:

(a) Use the company where you work, or that of a friend. It will have at least one legal counsel.
(b) Use reference books (I'll go into this a bit further on).
(c) Contact a professional organization representing your particular field of inquiry. There are associations in every field: an association of lawyers, of accountants. You can find associations in the yellow pages as well as in the white pages of your telephone book.
(d) Ask your banker.
(e) Don't overlook advice from friends, relatives, and co-workers who seem knowledgeable about these matters.

Early in my working career, it took me much too long to realize that I was sitting within fifty feet of an upturned cornucopia of resources. The first time I used my company as a source of guidance was in getting a car loan. My boss enthusiastically suggested that I talk with the firm's banker, which started the machinery. You've never in your life seen such incredible personal service over a matter as basic as a car loan for a Mustang!

Two qualifications for accepting any recommendations, corporate or otherwise, are (1) that you respect the source of the reference and (2) that you make sure your good Samaritans understand that it's *only* a reference—the final choice is yours, and some people get really possessive over giving references. For instance, you might want to say: "I'm in the market for a good tax attorney. Do you know one I should interview?" Also, I never take a reference's quality for granted. Everyone has a unique personality and a particular problem. Also, of course, the person whose help you're seeking may very well not know all there is to know about the referent's abilities.

3. *Secure a face-to-face interview.* This is the most crucial of the four steps. Understanding the purpose of the interview is all-important. Be perfectly clear in your mind about this. You are not seeking favors or begging assistance or otherwise improperly taking the Great Man's time. *You are hiring a professional*—buying his specialized skill—to assist you in achieving your desired goal.

I particularly enjoy the interview approach because it enables me to gather all the information I need in an upbeat fashion, sitting across the desk from someone. (If you do decide to use this person, the two of you will be working together in just this way, so the personal interview is in a sense a preview of what your relationship will be like.) After you've made up your list of three, call for appointments several days in advance. Be sure you raise the question of a fee in this initial telephone call. Should there be a fee for this brief preliminary meeting, make up your mind at this point whether or not you're willing to pay it. Speaking for myself, I would *not* be willing. Most reputable firms (and that includes legal firms) do not charge for a bona fide introductory meeting.

A word of caution here: Some very busy people may want to handle this question-and-answer session on the phone. Don't acquiesce. Press, however pleasantly, for a face-to-face meeting and don't be put off. Depending on the complexity of your problem or opportunity, the interview should take ten to fifteen minutes. Be prepared yourself and don't waste the professional's time—or your own. Remember, this is only an interview; your decision will come after you've seen all three of your candidates and gathered all the relevant information.

In an interview like this I use the following list of queries. (For special or unusual meetings I add pertinent questions or comments to it.) The seven points you want to be sure to cover are these:

—How old is the firm or institution?

—How many people are in the firm?

—In what areas do they specialize?

—What is the background of the person with whom you're talking? This would include schooling, degree, experience, and so on, and position with the firm. (*Always* ask for the person's card.)

—Who are his other customers or clients? If he can't or won't name names, at least try to find out what their profiles are like: companies or individuals, prominent or obscure, complex or simple.

—What are the precise fees or percentages involved?

—Does he have direct experience in your area of need?

Bear this in mind: The interview actually begins the moment you enter the offices. Surroundings often reflect the nature or capabilities of the occupant, so don't discount a questionable or disconcerting environment. Little things can sometimes tell you more than big things. Do the secretaries look capable? Are their desks in what a broker friend of mine calls "efficient disorder"? Or are they a hopeless welter of forms, unfiled letters, candy wrappers, and carbons—or, worse yet, swept utterly bare in that stark confession of inactivity? (I, for one, have never bought the propaganda about "a sterile desk equaling a fertile mind.") You want to feel good about a firm with which you're sharing your future. Pay attention to the vibes. Even the decor can be revealing. Don't fall for phony opulence.

Pay particular attention to the opening moments of your interview with your professional. This is when most people reveal their attitudes most clearly. A well-recommended accountant once kept a friend of mine cooling her heels in his outer office for over an hour, offered the most casual of apologies for this inconvenience, and then called in one of his secretaries and began giving her lengthy instructions on correspondence concerning other clients.

"I don't care how good they said he was," my friend told

me. "Anybody that rude and that disorganized isn't going to be reliable enough to handle *my* tax problems."

Nevertheless, be realistic. You may encounter someone who's simply too big to want to work with you. If a top real estate broker works only in the $100,000 bracket and your interest lies in $30,000 houses, a marriage probably won't be to the advantage of either of you. Don't take offense at this, or try to fight an already accomplished fact, hoping they'll change firm policy just for you. You can't afford such self-indulgence. Be sure to explain clearly and concisely your interest or situation at the outset, and then listen for their response. (Your explanation should cover who, what, where, how, and why.) This should tell you what you want to know. Your referent should start selling at this point. All people in the professional categories I've listed wear sales hats, too—they're in the service business, remember. The "sell" may be very direct, involving an analysis of situations similar to yours that the firm has solved effectively; or it may be very subtle—a discernible warmth of manner and a remark such as "I really look forward to hearing from you again about this."

These are the nuances you should weigh. Watch for attitude—alertness, clarity of expression (you need your professionals to be articulate), genuine interest in your problem. *People* run businesses, and human nature is the mainspring of the financial world just as in any other. Some years ago I interviewed a lawyer who suddenly broke off early in our interview to apologize for being in his shirt sleeves and without a tie, and then launched into a long, involved discourse on how he came to hate jackets and ties during army duty in New Guinea during World War II.

This digression told me several things about him I needed to know: He lacked the impersonal austerity you need in a lawyer. He had suddenly started thinking of me personally, as a reasonably well-dressed woman in his presence, not as a client with a rather complex problem that needed solving. Also, he was indecisive: If not wearing a jacket and tie embarrassed him, he should have put one on before the meeting, or he should have sat there tieless and not indulged in any apologies. Furthermore, he lacked discipline. He knew I had claims on my time as he did (or should have had) on his, but he chose to wander off down memory lane. And finally, he was dangerously self-centered: I had no interest at that moment in listening to his tales of the South Pacific, fascinating though they might have been, but *his* affairs interested him more than a prospective client's. These qualities simply do not combine to make the mixture you seek in legal counsel. Needless to say, I crossed him off my mental list and concluded our interview.

Trust your instincts. If a person rubs you the wrong way, after careful observation, my advice is to keep looking. There are plenty of other professionals out there; chances are you'll find someone with whom you can work in harmony. But don't be taken in by charm alone, either. It's a professional you want, not an escort or a friend.

Don't make a snap decision during the interview. Stick with your game plan. You may feel that a particular person or firm is the answer to your professional prayers; but in most cases you should give yourself time to make a dispassionate decision. A good exit line that doesn't imply any commitment on your part is: "If it should turn out that we'll be working together on this, what would the procedure be?" Accent the *should* if you like. You have left the situation open; now you are free to return home or to your office, make a comparison with the other two people you've interviewed, and come to your decision at your leisure.

A few minor points: If you feel uncomfortable at first about doing the interview alone, you may prefer to take someone along—who, by the way, should be fully briefed on *your* ground rules. You may present your companion as an assistant or business associate, if you like, to explain his or her presence. Two heads are frequently better than one (depending on the person and the situation, of course!), even if only one is doing the talking. Don't be afraid to jot down the professional's responses to your queries. If he takes offense at this, you don't want to retain him anyway, and this way you'll have notes to refer to when making your final decision. You may also want to use three-by-five file cards to check off your questions as you go along, though it's better to commit your basic seven points to memory. It frees you for other thoughts and observations.

4. *Decision for action.* This is your final step. Take your time, weigh the various attributes of your three candidates —expertise, personal interest, background, qualifications for your particular problem or enterprise—and make your decision. Make sure that you know exactly how you are to proceed: cost, time, the anticipated objective. Don't be embarrassed about putting it in writing, or asking your professional to do so.

A final note: Probably the most complex (and occasionally frightening) professional you'll be dealing with is your attorney. While doing research for this book I had a lengthy interview with Nancy Boxley Tepper, a lawyer with the law firm of Kindel and Anderson in Los Angeles, whom I asked how she would go about selecting an attorney. She said the best source for selection is the Martindale-Hubbell directory. It lists most lawyers in the United States and offers a comprehensive breakdown on the personnel within each firm, their areas of specialization, time in grade with the company, as well as confidential recommendations from other lawyers and judges. It can be found in most libraries. She also emphasized the importance of matching your need to the capability of the lawyer or firm. The advantage here, she stressed, was that while you should check with three references, a firm that specializes (or has a department that specializes) in, say, estate planning may in fact be able to save you a great deal of money simply because it won't have to refer everything to its research department.

If you move through these points diligently you will have made the best possible decision for yourself. And the pros you retain will know *they* are working for a professional.

You.

6 /

On Your Own: Becoming an Entrepreneur

This subject is dear to my heart, though it wasn't ever thus. The first time I heard that word *entrepreneur* was when a secretary ran into it on a dictation belt she was transcribing for her boss and asked me what in God's name it meant. I told her I didn't have the faintest idea. We consulted Mr. Webster, who informed us it was French and meant "one who assumes the risk and management of business; an undertaker (in the economic sense)."

Is there a particular reason a lot of women have trouble with that word? Are we subconciously afraid of it? At first glance it conjures up images of legendary men like Cecil Rhodes and his diamond mines, or Ferdinand de Lesseps and his Suez Canal, or the mighty railroad barons of our own West. Actually, of course, enterpreneurship can take a thousand and one forms, and some highly successful ventures have been achieved from very modest launching pads.

Women today need have no fear of entrepreneurship as an awesome, inaccessible world. Many enterprising women have moved from nine-to-five routines into careers that have proved lively, fulfilling, and profitable. When I started working I never dreamed I would have my own company, and I'm reasonably sure that other women to whom you'll be introduced in this book didn't either—not until they'd spent several years on corporate ladders or in institutional corridors, and then, for one reason or another, got the entrepreneurial "bug."

Take the case of Stephanie Winston, a former book editor who decided to turn her propensity for neatness and organization to her advantage. She left publishing, formed her own service company, and now counsels some of the industrial giants like IBM and Xerox on how to improve their filing systems—not to mention individuals such as doctors and other professionals who need help in straightening out the confusion in their offices. And then there's Barbara Boyle Sullivan, an ex-IBM executive who became so successful at running their women's affirmative action program that she formed Boyle/Kirkman Associates, which specializes in helping executives establish fair employment practices in their own firms—a creative spin-off indeed.

The most exciting thing about running your own company (either by yourself or with a partner) is that it is something you can love wholeheartedly, throw all your energies into: it's your baby. It can also be your prime investment vehicle as it is in my own case.

Even if you're not interested in this route to self-realization today, don't write it off. You may be in the not-so-distant future. Meanwhile, if you're somewhere deep in the corporate structure, you're learning a lot of valuable things about company organization, personnel, marketing—all the ingredients that make up the corporate pudding.

For me, launching your own business is like writing your own personal declaration of independence from the corporate beehive, where you sell bits of your life in forty-hour (or longer) chunks in return for a paycheck. Having participated in the founding of three new business concerns, I've discovered it's far more rewarding, both emotionally and financially, to work twice as long at something *you've* conceived and nurtured. Of course, let's face it, entrepreneurship has its frustration, even its downright terrifying moments. There have been times when Webster's definition of *undertaker* can take on rather grim overtones. It's true, you *may* be risking all that time and effort for nothing, but the potential rewards are worth it. There are times when I honestly think I'd rather own a pizza parlor than be one of a herd of vice-presidents in some mammoth corporation.

Going into business for yourself, becoming an entrepreneur, is the modern-day equivalent of pioneering on the old frontier. There are dangers, too, make no mistake about that; but there are just as many opportunities, and they are unique and exciting. Economist Peter Drucker hails the current period as a new age of the entrepreneur, which most experts feel has come about as a reaction to the bigness, the impersonal steamroller quality of corporate life, too monolithic to allow exploitation of the smaller opportunities that can be seized by one person or by a small and enterprising group.

Almost everyone, male or female, has a natural timidity about striking out alone, about giving up the security of a job in exchange for independence, trading the known for the unknown. But it's time that fear was laid to rest. It's time, too, to press outward from the traditional fields in which women, it was generally conceded, might excel simply because they were women. We all know how Elizabeth Arden and Helena Rubinstein achieved resounding success in the cosmetics industry. Now, however, women are expanding into less "feminine" areas. They are practicing—and succeeding—as architects, landscape gardeners, engineers, as well as in the more traditional roles of interior decoration and public relations.

Others are joining together to form new businesses connected with banking, credit, publishing, sports. A group of Detroit women during the past year has received a federal charter to organize the Feminist Federal Credit Union. And they've gone about it in a pragmatic way, charging 12 percent interest on loans and paying 6 percent interest on savings. In the words of one of the founders, "Some people think that we're so liberal and democratic we'll just lend money automatically, but we can't do that."

In weighing the risks of entering the marketplace on your own, you should take a long, hard look at your motivations for making such a move. Some of you may have the requisite ambition but not the special talents or instincts of an entrepreneur. Others may possess the mental and emotional equipment and still not welcome the total commitment to work that having your own company usually involves.

Nor is everyone cut out to be boss, especially boss of a fledgling outfit. This is a question you must examine with ruthless objectivity. For instance, you may find that you're not really at your best at initiating policy, that your strong suit is implementing decisions already made—in which case the entrepreneur's gambit is not for you.

Or you may discover that your strength lies in functioning as half of a team; in that case, you need to find a partner who is endowed with those skills you yourself lack or are not interested in developing. This will require some careful spadework. If you do decide to go into a business partnership with someone else, the only way you can truly evaluate the leader of a young and therefore highly risky venture is to ask for an extensive biography of the person involved—and then do a little quiet research on your own. If your prospective partner is the real thing, he or she will have no qualms about your checking, and that includes making a few telephone calls to previous or current associates as well as former firms. To put it crudely, don't be snowed or dazzled by the glitter of talent. Once you've checked the biography and made your queries, the glitter may prove to be duller or even decidedly tarnished. And if a prospective collaborator should refuse to give you a biography, or stalls about giving you one, drop the whole thing immediately.

My own experience in the area of joint enterprise was a very happy one. Beyond the exceptional imagination and drive that I could recognize for myself, Peter Stanton had a superlative track record. Nonetheless, you can be sure that I did some quiet research before committing myself. You are investing a sizable chunk of your life in a venture of this kind, and it behooves you to bring to the selection all the care and caution you would display in facing major surgery on your own body. The life you lose may be your own. Or you may win an entirely new and exciting future.

Your next step is to examine, every bit as impersonally, your reasons for leaving your present berth. They will tell you a lot about your capacity for striking out on your own. (Often the main reason is simple discontent.) You should run down the following possible motives for being dissatisfied as someone else's employee—dispose of the negative aspects of your projected move *before* shifting to the positive side of the ledger.

As a corporate employee, do you feel that there is a considerable gap between what you contribute toward your employer's financial success and the rewards you are receiving? Few companies, from my experience and that of many people I've talked with, are equipped to compensate fairly the *really* creative people on their payroll. They may pay bonuses, say, for patents-applied-for in their research laboratories, but the reward system is often based on the number rather than the commercial worth of such patents. A diligent and imaginative innovator can find herself ranked below mediocre hirelings who produce in quantity rather than quality.

Take the case of Evelyn Berezin, who had a Ph.D. in physics and worked for other companies for years while making important contributions in the data-processing field. Despite her inventive genius, she found that her sex was a severe handicap in achieving executive status.

"I could do a better job than most of the people around me," she said, "yet I could see that I was never going to get any further as an employee."

This despite the fact that she was an early arrival in the computer industry (she is now in her forties) and had started out by designing computers for a small company in New York; and later, while employed by a Connecticut firm, developed the first nationwide reservations system for United Air Lines.

A half-dozen years ago she abandoned her struggle to

persuade the corporate brass that she deserved a better shake, and with $375,000 in borrowed capital plus a very promising idea she founded Redactron Corporation on Long Island.

"I was convinced," she explained, "that something could be done to improve productivity by applying the computer to secretarial work. I estimated that by 1975 there would be four million typist-secretaries."

She then proceeded, along with three colleagues, to design an editing-typewriter system that produces typewritten copies of an original letter or document that has been recorded on a magnetic tape cassette. It was a field pioneered by IBM; Redactron was merely one of many smaller companies competing for the $200 million market.

Dr. Berezin put in a 14-hour day while mounting her challenge to the IBM empire. For several years Redactron's balance sheets were inscribed in red ink. One year the company lost $2.5 million on revenues of only $1.8 million. Sales then increased to the impressive annual rate of $7 million, and Redactron turned the corner when Sperry Rand's prestigious Remington Rand division contracted to buy $3.4 million worth of Redactron systems and sell them under the Remington Rand label.

Forming her own company, she said, was the only way she could fully capitalize on her talent and training. It took courage and initiative to step out of a well-paying job when she had just passed forty. But today she has not only the satisfaction of success, but the far deeper gratification of having won it on her own.

If you're a creative innovator who is disappointed in the way you've been rewarded, starting your own concern is worth the effort and risk, provided you can secure the marketing and financial expertise to match your abilities. But be honest with yourself. Many people simply can't function without the resources of a large corporation behind them. This is an important point for you to weigh. I know of all too many bankruptcy situations caused by big-company-type spending by infant firms.

Are you dissatisfied with your rate of promotion or your company's promotion policies? Many people feel that they are kept in one positon too long—and often enough they are—because those with seniority are largely preoccupied with keeping them on a lower rung of the corporate ladder, as a protection against losing their own status. This is particularly true of firms that do not have automatic retirement ceilings, where one aging owner or partner can destroy irreparably a firm's future by selfishly keeping out younger business talent. It's also particularly true of firms that still hold down women on principle—but there's no need to go into all *that* again.

Are you being defeated by office politics or by your company's practice of giving the plums to relatives? Many concerns are rife with water-cooler plots and corridor politicking. Some of the smaller firms are operated by members of one family, and non-kinfolk find the key executive spots closed against them.

Are you being stifled by a proliferation of red tape? Many companies are constituted like government bureaucracies and tend to manufacture as much needless paperwork as the products they are set up to make and market. There's nothing more frustrating to a woman with initiative than having to deal with people who insulate their own inadequacies with layers of red tape.

Are you being held back by educational snobbery? Many corporations are more interested in the degrees you've acquired, however intrinsically worthless or irrelevant they may be to job requirements, than in your real capacities. If you don't have a college degree, no matter how bright and ambitious you are, you'll find the avenues to advancement blocked at a firm of this kind. Even if you do have the degree, you may find it insufficiently helpful because it isn't from the "right" school. You may be pounding your head against the Ivy League wall. The girl beside you from Smith or Vassar is rapidly promoted for no particular reason except that she can speak the social language of the Princeton and Yale men in the executive suites.

All these reasons are valid enough for your being discontented with working for an employer who can't or won't perceive true excellence, no matter what its guise. They don't necessarily qualify you, though, to start your own business. They are *negative* arguments—they may merely signify that you should change passage on ocean liners, not take the helm of your own sloop.

If you feel you have more *positive* qualifications for going into business on your own, you should submit yourself to still another ruthless self-assessment. Your own character is as vital to such a new venture as any brilliant ideas you may have for staking out your own clearing in the woods.

Before taking the plunge, give strong consideration to the following positive factors:

1. *DRIVE.* You must possess a built-in self-starting mechanism. You aren't the type that needs to be pushed into action swiftly and decisively. You should have a compulsion for hard work and late hours. You must be willing, even eager, to sacrifice your spare time, sporting interests, evening activities.

2. *EXECUTIVE COMPETENCE.* You must have an exceptional capacity for gathering relevant information, deciding what is accurate and applicable, and acting on it. More often than not you must work with incomplete information, and chart the correct course just the same. The fear of making a mistake, resulting in failure to act decisively, has ended many a budding career. You *have* to be able to act decisively and take the consequences: The buck, truly, does stop here.

3. *MOTIVATION.* You've got to want success, to struggle unremittingly for it—and you must be resilient enough to bounce back from the setbacks, frustrations, or defeats that accompany most new ventures. You must be prepared to look upon your fledgling company as a child to be reared. It will take incessant care and thought, it may become an obsession; you should make its care and feeding a round-the-clock proposition. Many people simply cannot get that involved in something that seems to lack a personality. To the true entrepreneur, her company does have exctly that—a

personality, a marvelous life of its own that she has breathed into it and that must be nurtured.

4. *EXPERTISE.* You must immerse yourself in the product or service you're offering the market. You must know it inside and out—its strengths and its weaknesses, its potential, the dangers that threaten it—and you must know them better than anyone else in the world. You may think you can learn as you go, and profit from mistakes made through ignorance, but few embryo entrepreneurs have the capital to be able to afford that sort of on-the-job training. The clock ticks very fast in the business world, and the tuition fee demanded by the school of hard knocks can wipe you out before you're fairly started. Far better to have mastered the field you're planning to invade as an employee, privy to the trade secrets and methods of operation of someone already familiar with the field. That way you can acquire the requisite expertise *before* you launch your own canoe into the rapids.

5. *LEADERSHIP.* You must—you absolutely must—possess what can only be called leadership: that rare-as-rubies personal force that can resolve the clash of issues and personalities, pull others along with you, induce them to see things your way, to work their heads off in your young firm's behalf. You must inspire subordinates through force of example —work that hour or two longer than anyone else, have an answer when no one else does. Yes, there are times when you may have to simulate assurance when your own stomach is full of butterflies. In short, you have to inspire confidence and emulation 24 hours a day—or so it seems. All too often the chief of some new enterprise discovers at the moment of crunch that she lacks that ultimate clout or persuasiveness to forge a unanimity of view, and is forced to watch her fledgling company come apart at the seams.

6. *MANAGERIAL ACUMEN.* You should be a shrewd judge of character. You must be able to appraise the qualifications of prospective associates and lieutenants in the close personnel terms of your new venture. You must be able to winnow avarice from ambition, sycophancy or flattery from

loyalty, reflectiveness from lack of fiber. If you're entering into a partnership, your skills should dovetail, your personalities complement your partner's. Incompatible natures are fatal to a new business. You must analyze and measure the strengths and weaknesses of your prospective associates, and you must have the courage to obey that small inner voice if it murmurs to you that something in the personal equation is radically wrong.

7. *SENSE OF PERFECTION.* Finally, you should have an abiding contempt for the mediocre, the easy road, the gold brick; a boundless and inexorable sense of the possible beyond the impossible—that deep interior excitement at the challenge you throw in your own path, an all-consuming need to be the best you can be. Happiness is competence perfectly fulfilled.

.

These qualities are musts for any budding entrepreneur, and you'd better make sure you have most or all of them. A few of them can be learned, it's true, but the genuine entre-preneur feels them deeply without thinking about them. They are the thrust, the life force, that drives her.

A proud possessor of all these qualities and a ringing in-spiration to us all is Ruth Houghton Axe, who cut through the corporate jungle like a newly honed machete some years ago. Talk about your Renaissance man—this small, dynamic lady not only mastered her share of the business world but played the cello, excelled at chess, and was a crack shot with a rifle (on one occasion she hit every target in a shooting gallery).

She was an employee of the New York Telephone Com-pany when she married Emerson Axe, a securities analyst for the same firm. Undoubtedly the work she did for Ma Bell trained her to research a subject thoroughly—a skill that was to stand her in good stead in later years, when she would make herself an expert on any company she investigated, an au-thority who could be fooled neither by a tricky balance sheet nor by an overly optimistic annual report.

But her impatience with the ponderous corporation was all her own. She wanted, as she used to put it, to run her own shop. She persuaded her husband, a quiet, amiable, low-keyed man, into leaving New York Telephone and branching out with her as an investment counsel team (Axe-Houghton Financial Services), then on to mutual funds and industrial ventures (the Axe-Houghton Company). Emerson Axe was an excellent securities analyst in his own right, but Ruth was the emotional mainspring of their enterprises.

The valuable lesson of her career is that it was founded not simply on a dynamic personality—though she had that to spare—but on the incredible preparation she underwent before she made any important move. Homework was the key to her success in carving any new trail of opportunity. She would stay up half the night reading up on and analyzing some venture before Axe-Houghton took any part in its development. She made herself an expert on liquid fertilizers, for example, realizing their crucial importance to agricultural production around the world before most people had even heard of them. She acquired expertise—and startled the specialists—in such esoteric fields as mercury mining. She even went down into the mines herself. She mastered the history and chemistry of cement construction; she went into the field and analyzed the possibilities of lava-based cement, which is lighter than Portland cement and therefore cheaper to transport.

Ruth Axe was always willing to take a gamble, associates will tell you, but she never risked a flyer until she had informed herself on every aspect of the venture. And she had a healthy contempt for evasive rhetoric. Small, combative, with a volatile temperament and a furious impatience with anyone who tried to outfox her, she developed an uncanny ability to penetrate to the heart of any matter.

A sales executive who knew her well told me, "She ran the outfit like a candy store." He meant it as a compliment, too—in the sense that she made it her business to know every detail of the operations under its corporate umbrella better than any of the managers of the companies involved. She would write a check for a million dollars without flinching, but she went around switching off the lights in the offices at night (she was often the last to shut up shop) to cut down overhead. There is nothing kooky about this; she knew all too well, as any business chief of mission does, that profit margins are eroded by a vast array of small-leakage expenses.

I've given this mini-biography of Ruth Axe in detail because it highlights so beautifully the strategy any woman must evolve if she wants to clamber out of the wage-earning ranks. Her career is an entrepreneur's dream. She had determined at the earliest stages that she was not to be satisfied with a desk, a comfortable salary, and a pension from Ma Bell; she was determined to use her hard-won abilities for her own benefit. She knew the incomparable value of homework, and she could drive herself harder and longer than most people. She accepted the sacrifices involved: Her companies were her "children," and she gave them the requisite loving care. She saw that Emerson's talents and hers complemented each other—he in analysis, she in acquisitions and sales—and that their temperaments didn't clash. She mastered the expertise that gave her unquestioned authority in board meetings. She was not afraid to take large risks. And she had that overmastering need for achievement, for perfection in her own world. Consequently, she won all the marbles.

There are other qualities usually possessed by successful entrepreneurs, and you should decide whether they are or are not part of your psychological makeup.

The desire for a personal fortune may rise very gradually to the surface of your consciousness. You may have worked for years at a satisfactory salary, with adequate prospects for promotion, but you're reaching the age when your expenses are increasing (your children may be approaching college age) and you have to think about security in the long term; or you may be a young, single woman who's decided marriage is not for you; or you may have been recently widowed. That's when many women find themselves taking out a subscription to the *Wall Street Journal* and avidly reading the success stories of new enterprises; that's when all that Horatio Alger stuff no longer seems so corny.

If you're in any of these categories, you may start comparing your own potential as an independent operator with that of other people who have made good on their own, and you may be wondering why you shouldn't get some of those goodies at the top of the money tree for yourself instead of your employer.

The desire for fame may be another motivation factor. If you're the entrepreneurial type, you may be irked by the fact that up till now, everything you've accomplished redounds to the greater glory of a trademark or family name. (Why Eastman Kodak, Estée Lauder, Diane von Furstenberg, instead of *your* name?) The thrill of seeing your own name in a newspaper advertisement or on an office sign, or hearing it in a television commercial, might not be the overriding factor in your determination to start your own company. But you obviously have a healthy ego, and you'll derive a definite satisfaction from a separate and highly visible identity.

Another strong drive is the pure joy of winning. Only as entrepreneurs can we fully experience the exhilaration of outdoing the competition. The excitement of commercial combat, the delight in battling with your wits (and winning), the fierce pride in matching yourself against your rivals may provide you with more satisfaction than anything else in starting your own business. Thomas Alva Edison never demonstrated any aversion to piling up a fortune on his many inventions, but he once said: "I don't care so much about making my fortune as I do for getting ahead of the other fellows." Helena Rubinstein wrote of the intense joy she felt in outmaneuvering and surpassing the competition.

Success can be sweet, especially when attained on your own terms. Mary Wells Lawrence, who started out as a brilliant young copywriter, used her executive ability and administrative talent to rise as an account executive and eventually put together one of the ten biggest advertising agencies in the country in Wells, Rich and Green. Yet the source of her astonishing success lay in her ability to function as a pro in the financial community, not just in advertising. She personally made $3 million from her public issue, earns more than $426,000 a year, and has just proposed to the Securities and Exchange Commission that she buy back the outstanding shares of her company—in effect doing a reverse public issue called "going private," which would mean that she could own, once again, all or most of her firm. This is obviously a highly dramatic and sophisticated way to make money; and it is my bet that she will make a substantial profit on *all* these transactions. Trim, elegant, and attractive, she is radiant proof of a woman's ability to make the most of an enormous personal talent.

There is one last factor to be weighed in determining whether you should join the ranks of the entrepreneurs, and that is the personal one. Such a move, you must realize, will complicate relationships. You will have less time for people close to you, less occasion for the emotional comforts offered by and to children, lovers, friends.

If you're a married woman and value your marriage, you must be assured of the wholehearted support of your mate. If you're divorced or widowed and have children emotionally or financially dependent on you, you'll have to take their needs and natures into account. People who've been through it say that being married both to a person and to a company you've founded can be one of the most demanding of experiences, taxing all your reserves. There is the price of success to be considered, as well as its rewards. But with this one as with all the other factors I've discussed, only *you* can make the decision.

7 /

Creating Your
Business Plan

If you intend to establish your own business, you must have a clear blueprint far in advance. A business plan, in fact, should be the first step you take. It's vital, because it forces you to work your way through those demanding questions: Will it work? *How* will it work? Will I make any money at it? You might get by without a plan, for a little while, if you're famous and terribly rich. But of course the terribly rich are too smart to do anything without a plan.

Your business plan has other values beyound self-appraisal. It forms the basis for presentations to banks from whom you may need to borrow money or to firms that might invest in your business (they're called venture capital firms). It may also be used to persuade suppliers to grant you credit, to convince prospective customers of the viability of your enterprise and the advisability of placing orders with you. And, obviously, it can be used to attract private investors.

Whenever you make a "money presentation," for any reason, you need a business plan. Money people are naturally impressed with words and numbers—facts around which they can form a decision. It's always difficult to make a decision involving money based on oral presentation. As you read this chapter, think of your plan's wider uses—such as the next time you need a loan from your bank or an addition to your house.

Your business plan, in fact, is your key selling tool to the world until you can stand on your own financial feet, a scenario of what you hope for and believe you can accomplish —what I refer to as the "who, what, why, when, and how much" plan. It should answer the tough question you'll probably be asked more than once: "What have you got to offer that can't be found elsewhere in the marketplace from an established firm?"

To provide an example, I'll quote from one business plan I put together for a proposed venture called Cortrex Corporation, on which I sought to raise $250,000 in financing. The project never was pushed to fruition (instead, I started a totally different company with Peter Stanton) but the money people I showed it to gave it high marks. If you've never seen a business plan, let me give you a quick picture. The Cortrex plan was 14 pages long, and the table of contents read as follows:

TABLE OF CONTENTS

At the outset, I explained that Cortrex was designed to

become a "leading producer of audio cassettes for the fields of business and finance. . . . The company plans to create, produce, and distribute informational, educational, and training cassettes as well as to market cassettes produced by other companies. The company projects a profitable posture by the eighth month of operation with achievable sales increases projected for years two and three."

I then explained that the cassette field promised rapid growth, that the sales of cassettes had leaped from 5 million in 1966 to an expected 200 million by 1975. To bridge the normal, non-income-producing months of initial operation, Cortrex had begun negotiations with a cassette-producing firm to distribute a number of their tapes and "allow Cortrex to realize substantial sales by the third month of operation." (It's important, obviously, to indicate to prospective financial backers that, as a young struggling company, you will have revenue coming in as quickly as possible.) I then listed a number of subjects on which Cortrex planned to produce tapes. Among them were business and management topics, and there were several series on women's opportunities as they related to business and industry, on the women's consumer market, and on self-help for career or working women to advance in their fields.

As you can see, the business plan anticipates the general questions outsiders are going to ask. Few people ever know companies the way you know your own.

Since it's essential to prove that you know just what the market is, and how to tap it, I then outlined our marketing plan. Cortrex would use both direct-mail campaigns and space advertising. "For the business tapes, four-part direct-mail pieces will be sent to small and middle-sized companies with less emphasis placed on lists such as the *Fortune* 500 [*Fortune* magazine's annual listing of the 500 largest industrial corporations]."

Tie-ins with other companies to distribute Cortrex's cassette programs when they became available were also cited, with the explanation that "these companies will afford Cortrex a highly trained, professional concept sales force to market its products."

To provide as complete and fair a picture as possible of the field I proposed to enter, I listed some of the leading competitors, up to and including such companies as Time-Life, with an estimated sales volume of $2 million a year in their tape division, and the Success Motivation Institute, with a $12 million estimated annual sales volume.

To indicate the source of the material to be recorded on our tapes, I reported that Cortrex was "in final negotiations with an author who, it believes, brings great versatility to Cortrex. The author was previously director of personnel training for a leading financial institution. . . . Other authors have been tentatively selected for specific topics but will not be approached until financing for the company has been concluded."

One of the two recording studios in the Los Angeles area would be selected to produce the master tapes. "We do not anticipate doing our own in-house tape duplication until the fourth month, at which time the volume will warrant the purchase of a cassette duplicator," I further explained. "The price difference between in-house duplication and outside duplication is approximately 20 cents per tape, or 15 percent."

This business plan was designed simply to demonstrate that I knew the field I was proposing to enter, how to invade the market, and how and what to produce.

The main thing here is to be concise. Come right to the point and stay on it. Avoid blowzy generalities and phony phrases like "expanding possibilities." Nothing will cool the interest of a prospective investor faster than that kind of verbiage. Be factual, straightforward, and as brief as you sensibly can.

Equally interesting to prospective backers, of course, is the precise way in which the financial management of the projected company will be handled. This comes under the heading of "The Financial Plan" and must be very carefully considered. Mine read as follows:

As the 1972 financial forecasts show, Cortrex requires capital of $250,000 to realize its program. For this equity investment, the Company is prepared to issue 40 percent of its common stock to the investment group. The additional financing required to realize the expansion goals will be supplied from profits earned and bank credit which should be available to the Company after its first year of operation.

The earnings forecast project an efficient operation run with extreme frugality. Capital expenditures will be minimized at the outset in order to preserve the Company's capital.

I then outlined my qualifications to be chief executive officer of Cortrex, including my previous career and my experience as sales manager and a corporate officer of Infonics, which manufactured cassette-tape duplicators, and listed an advisory board of three leading figures in the audio-visual field.

At the back of the brochure I laid out the "earnings forecast" for the first year of operation. You have to be realistic in making such a projection. You have to know that your prospective backers know that a new company isn't going to take off like a rocket in its first 12 months of corporate life.

In my forecast I projected a gross margin (the difference between sales and cost of sales) of $102,262. Offsetting this was a total of $125,541 in selling expenses, salaries, and fees, rent, phone and utilities, postage, travel, office supplies, insurance, and contingencies. Thus I forecast a net loss of $23,279 for the first year of operation—modest under the circumstances, but realistic when you consider the fact that I planned to keep operating expenses to a minimum.

The second section of the earnings forecast, which naturally reflected a more cheerful attitude, ran as follows:

	Year Two	*Year Three*
Net sales	$370,000	$585,000
Cost of sales	144,000	222,000
Gross margin	226,000	363,000
Selling and G & A expense	178,000	282,000
Net profit before taxes	48,000	81,000
Income taxes	18,000	34,000
Net earnings	30,000	47,000

My particular prospectus offered a cheerful picture, yes, but not overly optimistic considering the growth industry I was proposing to enter.

I also included a "balance sheet forecast," and a "source and application of funds forecast" for the first year of operation.

I would not claim that my prospectus for Cortrex was the perfect model of a business plan, but it did contain the essential ingredients, and could be effectively applied to many different kinds of business ventures.

I bound the copies of my prospectus in good-looking black covers complete with a table of contents and page numbers. Each copy was also dated and numbered, and I kept a log telling who had received them and when. It's not a particularly good idea to have them floating around.° The quality of presentation is particularly important in a prospectus, which must, of course, be neat, clear, and professionally typed and photostated. The presentation is representing you; it's your selling tool. It therefore should look as good as you and your potential investment opportunity.

If you start up your own business, even if you don't have to seek large-scale financing, you should draw up a business plan—not only as a prospectus for anyone you hope to interest in the venture, but, just as important, for your own guidance and self-analysis.

° In fact, the SEC has a rule to the effect that you have to file an expensive "public issue" prospectus when the number of prospective investors reaches 35.

8 /

Launching Your
Own Business

Once you've definitely decided to go on your own and begin the process of founding a business, you'll soon learn that when successful business people say that "success costs money" they aren't being simpleminded. The biggest problem the budding entrepreneur usually faces is her lack of financial expertise.

She may have a brilliant idea for a new and needed product, she may be a crack operator in the sales field, she may be a highly capable administrator, but the new company head rarely understands that the more success she hopes to achieve, the more financing she'll need. If your business takes off on a sudden upward trajectory, you'll have to find financing for a bigger inventory, more accounts receivable, an increased payroll, and perhaps larger quarters. You'll have a money crunch brought on by success rather than failure.

When Infonics' sales increased 400 percent, Peter Stanton and I were faced immediately with the problem of how to raise an amount of money substantial enough to keep pace with such rapid expansion. We had two choices: Debt financing and equity financing. Debt financing is similar to securing a loan from a bank; equity financing means giving up a part of your corporation in exchange for funding. We chose the second approach; in exchange for a healthy chunk of the company we received over $1 million and Infonics became a publicly held corporation. Again, the more successsul you are, the more money you will need.

Recently I did some consulting with two women who told me they were talking with the Small Business Administration about a $150,000 loan. It quickly became obvious that it was going to be enough to last them only nine months. I suggested they increase their proposal by a least another $100,000 and then went on to explain why. You must plan on at least an 18-month period to get your new company working, whether it's a glass boutique or a motor scooter plant, to get your starting problems resolved and become sufficiently stable.

That's why, as I've stressed earlier, it's so important to develop a sound relationship with a bank well in advance. Make yourself visible to your bank officer. Your character, and your ability to convey its essence to the person who has to decide on business loans, will be a crucial factor in determining whether or not you get the money to expand in step with your increased volume of business.

When Peter Stanton and I were looking for a new business after selling Infonics, we surveyed the prospects of 132 companies, as well as an equal number we turned down on the phone. Many of them were faltering, or they wouldn't have been inviting outside participation. The one thing they had in common, we found, was a scary lack of financial expertise at the top. One company in the insurance education field, for example, would merrily ship out material without bothering to make sure it would even be paid for!

A problem experienced by virtually all beginning entrepreneurs is the necessity of cutting expenditures right down to absolute essentials. One firm we looked at, that was in debt a cool $250,000 after one year of operation, had more than $16,000 invested in office furniture alone. It was the most beautiful potential bankruptcy in town.

Don't bedazzle yourself with the idea that a flashy front, a bold splash in the marketplace, a blast of advertising trumpets is going to clear your path like a bulldozer. Too often a person starting a business will be eager to impress friends and associates instead of putting the emphasis on the customer, will sink too much money in office furniture and draperies, fancy brochures and so on. Until the money comes rolling in, it may be a good idea to have a low-cost service outfit type your letters rather than hire an expensive secretary, or do your own decoration and cleaning (without letting people know you're doing it). In any case, it's never a good idea to let yourself be carried away with the grandeur of your new position.

Far more important than putting up a flamboyant front is carefully balancing your income against expenses, and conserving your funds for the expensive process of searching out that market for your product or services (unless, of course, you've done the classic thing—gone into competition with your former employer—in which case you know that market as well as he does). Instead of jumping into a marketplace, I've started and ended at least three companies in the *business plan* stage. If you *can't* pull it together in a few pages, don't waste your time trying to make it work in the market. Before you go into business for yourself you should be equipped with a complete financial forecast for at least a year in the future. If you lack financial training, you may need expert assistance in this sector.

You'll find that you'll incur enough expenses without indulging in luxuries. Stationery and business cards are a must, but keep the letterhead simple and dignified. If your firm or product lends itself to an exciting trademark, colophon, or logotype, such as the famous script of General Electric or the Mercedes-Benz tricon, well and good—visual impact and identification are worth millions of words. But choose one that's simple and tasteful.

You'll need the services of an outside accountant. Usually you would be well advised to choose a certified public accountant—that is, one who has passed the difficult CPA examination given by your state. Accountants range from the small one-man professional around the corner to the "Big Eight,"—the eight largest accounting firms—the biggest of which is Peat Marwick Mitchell and Company. The fee is generally in direct proportion to the size and prestige of the accounting firm, and you will have to balance your accountant's knowledgeability with what you can afford to spend on his services.

A word of caution: I've found that all too often accountants are numbers manipulators rather than people who truly understand the significance of numbers. This understanding normally is more likely to be found in people who are financially oriented and trained rather than in accountants, but few of these seem to practice as independent professionals. You must therefore make a real attempt to judge how knowledgeable your accounting adviser really is in the meaning of numbers as opposed to their manipulation.

A decision will have to be made immediately, of course, as to what sort of legal form your business will take: a proprietorship (one-person operation), a partnership, or a corporation.

Incorporating, which requires the services of a lawyer, will usually cost from $700 to $1,000. The primary reason for incorporating is to avoid personal liability. For example: if a caller at your office falls over a misplaced chair and breaks his leg, he can sue the corporation for damages but not the incorporator. If you take out a loan, the corporation—not you personally—is responsible, although a bank will usually make you personally guarantee the corporation's loan (this is standard bank practice in the case of small, privately held companies). If the corporation goes bankrupt, your personal assets and property can't be seized for repayment of debts. And there's another advantage in incorporation: If you have a partner and he obligates the company beyond its resources, you may have to make good for the debts he incurred on behalf of the partnership. The creditors will look to whichever partner has the greater ability to pay, regardless of which partner incurred the obligation.

One drawback to incorporating is that you have to pay corporate income taxes as well as a personal income tax on dividends. Under certain circumstances this can be avoided under Subchapter S in the Federal Tax Code, which allows the income of a corporation to be taxed directly to the stock-holders. If you do not elect the Subchapter S route, the corporation will have to pay corporate taxes on all its net income; when it declares dividends to you, its stockholder, you will then *again* have to pay personal income tax on those dividends. This is double taxation and can readily be avoided through a Subchapter S election. Your accountant can tell you about it.

If you issue stock in your compay, you should investigate Section 1244 of the Internal Revenue Code, which provides that, if you've taken a loss on your stock by selling it below your original cost or by having it become worthless, you can deduct up to $25,000 a year from your income. Your attorney will advise you on the rules and regulations governing the issuance of the stock, which differ from state to state. Usually he will take care of the legal details of incorporation.

Another question to be given serious consideration is whether you should buy a going concern rather than starting one yourself. Buying can be attractive—after all, someone else has done the groundwork. You might also seek to acquire the unprofitable division of a large company. However, this is a *highly* sophisticated area of finance, it takes considerable capital, and its ramifications are beyond the scope of this book. Suffice it to say that there are hefty bargains in this field, especially right now—but only for those who have the expertise that such a venture demands.

Be conceptually creative: Fit your prospective business venture to your own strengths. As the chief executive of such an enterprise, you should be well rounded enough to understand the sales, manufacturing, engineering, purchasing, financial, and accounting aspects of the operation. Your main strength as an entrepreneur will probably be in one of those areas, possibly two, but you've got to be able to deal with problems affecting all of them. If you are deficient in one or more of those areas, you should seriously consider taking in a partner or partners who have the ability to cover them.

Tailoring your talents to the product or service you'll be offering is also worth serious consideration. The amount of knowledge and/or experience you'll need for supplying a product will generally be more than you'd have to demonstrate if your venture dealt in a service. Manufacturing electric motors is more complicated than running a cleaning and dyeing establishment (though cleaning and dyeing has its complexities and pitfalls, too).

The main thing is to discover *in advance* what area or areas you're deficient in. So many enterprises crash because of a flaw in the business background of the founder which is discovered too late. Cover your deficiencies before you start operating. It's too late once the wheels are turning over. It's amazing how swiftly a financial shoestring can become frayed and snap.

Look for businesses within businesses. An architect who wants to branch out on her own could go into interior design, or specialize in designing convention booths, or coordinate the engineering and landscaping for a condominium complex.

Often a feasible scheme can be found more or less in your own back yard. Take the case of Dorothy Sarnoff, who used her theatrical background to start courses for people who needed training in public speaking. She recognized the need of a product to go with the service she was offering. That product was a book, *Speech Can Change Your Life*, which not only was successful in its own right but brought in as clients the people who read it. Another example is that of Jean Nidetch, the founder of Weight Watchers, who took advantage of the fact that she had been fat as a girl and made a career out of helping other people conquer their weight problems. Her angle was to combine dieting with the reinforcing principles of Alcoholics Anonymous. She held the first meetings of her group in her own home; eventually, with her husband and a friend brought in as a business manager, she launched her franchise system on an international basis. Having capitalized on her sales ability, plus a brilliant idea, she made a resounding success of the venture.

Franchises can be profitable, provided you make sure you're not dealing with fly-by-night operators who will take your money and leave you high and dry. You have to assure yourself, too, that the franchise offers a product or service that will prove attractive in your community; it has to fit *local* needs. The advantage of a franchise is that you have your business charted for you, with every detail of the operation laid on—including site selection (though not always), cooperative advertising, and the provision of supplies. Some highly successful franchise operations are Kentucky Fried Chicken, McDonald's and Postal Instant Press (PIP).

As your business gets rolling, you should take full advantage of the fact that there will be many people eager to help you on your way. It's downright amazing how many friends a struggling young business attracts—provided you're not too proud to accept their help and don't resent what sometimes may seem a patronizing attitude.

Don't hesitate to seek advice, a commodity that many knowledgeable people are pleased to offer. A successful businessman or businesswoman can help you over many hurdles, spot defects in your method of operating, save you the trouble and pain of making your own mistakes by recalling theirs. Such a person can often widen your potential market by giving you referrals, suggesting people or companies that can use your product or service.

Suppliers are a vital source of help. If you need credit for supplies, lay it on the line. If you're completely candid with them, you'll convince them that they're taking a risk on a person of integrity. Pay their bills promptly the first time around to establish both credit and credibility. (If you can't you should not have gone into business in the first place.) Suppliers will be eager to help you succeed. You're a customer, after all, and your success will contribute to their profits. And they, too, can provide invaluable marketing tips.

Bankers, for much the same reason, can also take a friendly interest in getting your venture off the ground. Again you must establish credibility, especially if you're operating on a shoestring. To guide a banker whose help you need, compile a *pro forma* statement listing your liabilities as well as your prospects for success. As I've mentioned earlier, bankers are vitally interested in the success of new ventures, despite their hard-nosed reputation. They don't spend millions of dollars on institutional advertising just to attract the finance committees of General Electric and United States Steel. Some of these very large banks have a small business investment company, know as an SBIC, whose specific purpose it is to make risk investments in small companies. Frequently these investments take the form of loans convertible into stock. There are, in addition, many SBICs not owned by banks, which may provide a source of funds for a small enterprise. Scrutinize their contracts carefully with your attorney before committing your company.

Distributors, who provide wholesale outlets for a particular industry, can also be helpful to the beginning entrepreneur, especially by coming up with pricing and marketing suggestions. They can help you avoid making disastrous mistakes in overpricing for your potential market, which will keep you in a competitive position with any rivals you may have.

Educators should not be ignored as a source of inspiration and guidance. Many professors are business consultants on the side. You may find their professional advice too expensive, but there are other advantages in keeping in touch with the faculty of the nearest university or college. There are benefits on both sides. From you they learn how technology that was developed in their studies or laboratories can be applied in your field. From them you can obtain technical and financial guidance of all kinds, often free. Don't be shy about seeking advice from the academics; true, they may sometimes seem impractical, but select what you can make best use of from their theoretical ideas, and ignore the rest.

There are details in the process of making your enterprise stand out which may seem minor but can nonetheless be very important: the design of your company's logotype, answering business correspondence promptly, overseeing the way the telephone is answered. I am not recommending pretentiousness in conceiving a corporate image; I *am* recommending that you put your best foot forward. Call it professionalism, if you're tired of the word "image."

If you have a worthwhile product or service to sell, you owe it to yourself to enhance it in any legitimate way that applies—packaging, merchandising ingenuity, advertising, promotion. Otherwise you won't be able to compete successfully with rivals who may offer an inferior product or service that is merchandised well.

The aura with which you make your venture attractive to the buying public will help to clear an initial place in the market. But it's only a means to a desired end, a tactic rather than a strategy. As Robert Townsend has put it, "Image is not a goal. It's a by-product. *A good image has to be earned by performance.*" The real goal, he stresses, is "customer satisfaction, and shareholder satisfaction."

As any good coach will tell you, one invariably learns more from losing than from winning. Looking back on my own mistakes, I want to stress several points that may seem self-evident but are for that very reason often neglected.

If you're determined to start your own business, you should first try to make certain that you'll derive more profit from it (while working harder, of course, and being assailed by all the slings and arrows of your independent status) than you would from a salaried job. Profit, rather than ego gratification, should take priority. (However, the real satisfaction of entrepreneurship has its own priceless value.)

Don't try to be something you're not. If you're trained in engineering, don't insist on taking over the marketing phase of your operation. If you're not detail-oriented, make sure you associate yourself with someone who will see to it that invoices go out on time and are paid. Genius, Carlyle said, is the infinite capacity for taking pains. No matter how much drive and ingenuity you possess, you can be crippled by those little "self-evident" things.

Finally, I want to mention fear, and the fear of fear. Eden Ryl, who operates a New York training and management firm, faces this issue head on: "Failure is only temporary—never permanent—unless you let it be. Everyone is afraid of something." In the 200 motivational seminars she conducts every year, Miss Ryl emphasizes the fact that "you create your own fears, so you can eliminate them. . . . Be willing to change your attitude."

Amen to that. You must conquer fear of failing or of realizing your fullest potential by analyzing it. You'll find most of the time that the fears are only the shadows of an attitude. A negative attitude. A fear of breaking old patterns. You'll find that the world of the entrepreneur is not some trackless wilderness to be crossed—that it can be a highroad to self-fulfillment.

9 /

How to Get Your Own Way: The Art of Negotiation

Bargaining, from the days of the horse traders and peddlers, is ingrained in the American business tradition. Few of us realize this. To the modern American woman, however, there is something repugnant or demeaning about haggling. It's something she thinks happens only in the souks of Middle Eastern cities. The result, of course, is that the American woman traveler is usually regarded abroad as a prime sucker.

Well, that image may suffice for picking up trinkets in Casablanca. Here at home you'd better be prepared to bargain, haggle, browbeat, and outmaneuver the best of them; otherwise your prospects of success are limited. Perhaps negotiating can best be characterized by the famous words from the Sermon on the Mount: "Ask and you shall receive."

Actually negotiation touches almost every area of your life, whether you're contacting your neighborhood bank for a loan, signing a lease, buying or selling a house or car, or seeking a new job or a raise. Most of us are negotiating every day of our lives. But not all of us are aware that we're negotiating. It's just silly to ignore this fact. If you are being interviewed for a new job you may be able to secure as much as $1,000 a year more, simply by using sound negotiating techniques and holding your ground at the crunch. Nationwide seminars on the subject are now being conducted in recognition of its crucial nature in today's business world.

This chapter, then, will offer a very short course on the fine art of negotiation, the strategy and tactics involved. Some of what I say may sound hard, even cynical; but believe me, it is knowledge earned through sometimes bitter experience. (Profit from my wounds, if you will!) More and more you'll find, as I did, that the success of any enterprise depends to a fantastic degree on your ability to get your own sweet way. And if that way happens to be mistaken or unsound, you could very well sabotage your venture at the outset.

Let's begin with that most common (and vexing) situation: asking the boss for a raise. It's no secret that a lot—an awful lot—of women are doing jobs worth a good deal more than they're getting paid for. The issue is how to get paid what you're worth. Are you? I've been on both sides of this barrier, both as employer and as employee. It was only after I became an employer that I realized what chances I'd passed up as an employee—how strong my essential position had been and how foolishly I'd failed to take advantage of it.

So here you are. You want a raise, and your employer has to be convinced that you deserve one (or more than one). One of the basic planks in negotiation is casting a cool eye on the overall picture: You must establish your own position first. Begin by asking yourself these questions:

1. How valuable am I to the firm?
2. What would it cost in time and money to replace me, train someone else to replace me?
3. What is the worst that could happen if my employer said no?
4. Can I get a job somewhere else? How easily? Do I have contacts in other firms in the same field?
5. Does my company or department have the available funds to grant a raise?
6. Are others in my company being paid more than I for the same job? Am I performing more than one job?
7. What is my relationship to my boss?

8. What have I done for my employer or company lately (cut costs, increased production, raised sales, whatever)?

After you've asked yourself these questions and have come up with good answers to them, you're ready to develop your game plan:

1. *Try to make your presentation to your boss outside his office.* If possible, invite him to lunch, or meet him in your office or the conference room. This shifts the interview out of the old "boss's office," chief-subordinate pattern and can lighten the psychological pressure on you a bit.

2. *Have your reasons for a raise carefully defined.* If you don't feel comfortable saying them out loud, write them out and hand them to him during the meeting. But it's much better to talk it out—the spoken word is usually softer and more pliable than the written one.

3. *Determine exactly how large a raise you want and how much it would cost the company by the hour and month and year.* This is important. You must know *precisely* what you're talking about. Then ask for slightly more than you expect, in order to leave room for negotiating.

4. *Be sure you suggest the amount of the increase, not your boss.*

There are a number of tactics that have been used very effectively (on me, I might add) within this framework. One, of course, is the power play of telling your employer you've received an offer for a similar position with another company, for more money. This can give you excellent leverage—unless, of course, it makes him so mad he gives you your walking papers. This last point is one you must weigh very carefully before your meeting.

The other approach—not recommended, just mentioned in passing—is the third-party negotiating method. This is where you let it be known through your boss's secretary or some other key employee that you've had another offer and you "don't know what to do about it." Be sure to tell your intermediary the subject is confidential. If he or she is a good, loyal type, and you yourself are a valued employee, the word will get out, and you'll get your raise, for one reason: The boss won't want to lose you.

Another tip: Don't let resentment at being passed over make you so angry that you defeat your own purpose. In any firm, but especially in a fledgling one, it's possible that your boss is simply too busy or harried to remember when it's salary review time for you. He or she may even be waiting to be reminded. Executives often like to see signs of aggressive spirit, a sense of inherent worth, in their subordinates. My very capable assistant at Infonics, Inc., Barbara Hauser, was always having to give me a gentle reminder at review time. There was never any question in my mind that she *was* due for a raise, but I was working my head off at the time or away in the field, and if she hadn't reminded me she might have gone for several months without her due increase.

Obviously, these suggestions are designed to give you leverage, but they should be used only if you've been a "good and faithful servant." If you haven't you could end up feeling very embarrassed—and unemployed. Be sure your self-analysis is carefully and accurately thought out.

Now let's talk about negotiating in general. If you're starting your own business, you'll find yourself bargaining at the very outset with a landlord, suppliers, prospective customers, the people you will hire. If you're buying out an established firm, the amount you'll pay for the takeover may actually determine the fate of your venture. To put it bluntly, you will probably be negotiating with people more experienced at it than you are.

The main principles involved in the art of negotiation (aside from the realization that if you don't get your way, or as much of it as is reasonable, the other fellow will get his and you'll be sorry) apply to many situations:

1. Establish credibility as your first move. Make the other

person realize that you are aboveboard, trying to be constructive rather than trying to take unfair advantage. Don't be too tough or drive too hard a bargain, at least in the beginning; no one wants to work with a "sharp operator."

2. Always try to hold the negotiating session on your turf —your office or your home. That's where you feel comfortable and the other person feels out of place. You won't always have this choice, but when you do, take it.

3. Get concessions from the other side as early as possible. For example, if you're negotiating for a lease, ask the lessor for fresh blacktopping on the drive or new storm sashes —anything, however small, that might induce him to make a concession. It will set a precedent for the meeting. Ease him into the habit of saying yes.

4. Again, as in salary negotiations, ask for more than you realistically can expect to get. This leaves you room for maneuver, to advance alternatives or counterproposals, and to establish a fallback position.

5. As the bargaining proceeds, give the other side some small victories; put up only a token fight on certain minor points.

6. Keep psychological motivations in mind. Occasionally they can be more important than monetary ones. When someone sells his own house, for example, he may want to sell to a sound, reputable family as much as he wants to attain top dollar.

7. Early on in the exchanges, ask a question to which you already know the answer. If the other party corroborates it, good. If not, you've learned something very valuable: your opposite number is either misinformed on that point or is not leveling with you. You will need to tread with some care.

8. Leave the other side room for maneuver, too. A peremptory or inflexible stance delivered too early can destroy any chance for the give-and-take that is the essence of any negotiation. A bargaining session should build slowly, like a friendship.

9. Always have an associate present during negotiations if

you possibly can, if another's presence is relevant to your particular kind of business. (Obviously, some negotiations are conducted by phone, and some are best conducted alone.) If your partner cannot make the meeting for any reason, postpone it. You may *think* you're the equal of any number of opponents, but it's not that simple. Two heads are often better than one, and unless you have a fabulously retentive memory, you won't recall everything that was said, and *how* it was said. Having at least one associate with you can double the persuasive power you can muster. Don't neglect to learn who your adversaries will be, and how many will be there on the other side of the table. If they have five on their side, you should bring at least three to yours.

Another advantage to having at least one ally is that it enables you to observe the "body language" of the opposition. While you're talking and arguing, your confederate can be watching. Books have been written on the subject of detecting, through physical signs and movement, what the other fellow is thinking. The crossing of arms or locking of fingers, a jiggling foot and scores of other twitches and gestures have their significance for the experienced observer.

10. When basic agreement has been established, put it in writing, even if it's not the ultimate, refined version. Getting something in writing effects an immediate commitment. Don't necessarily wait for fancy typing. Handwriting is perfectly valid, and both parties should sign then and there. In many negotiations this principle will apply. People, being human, change their minds; many an agreement has broken down while the parties waited for neatly typed copies of it in quintuplicate.

11. After an agreement has been reached, stop the meeting, stop selling, stop talking, *shut up*. You already have what you want. Don't risk fouling it up. As salespeople have learned to their sorrow, many a sale has been lost after it's been made simply by talking on and on and on.

The most careful preparation possible is essential to success. You must do your homework: Have a blueprint of what you hope to achieve, and what you need to secure as an absolute, non-negotiable minimum. It may suit your purposes to keep a check list of your objectives in front of you at the bargaining table—but don't, for heaven's sake, let the other side see it, any more than you'd give an opponent a glimpse of your hand in a card game. A better course is to commit to memory your objectives, alternative offers, fallback positions: what you *must* gain, what you *can* concede. Facts, and your command of them, are vital; the more securely you hold them in your mind, the greater ease of manner and facility of argument you'll bring to the table.

Let's take a relatively simple example. You're buying a house. The asking price is $55,000 and the best you can do is $47,000. Get out your pencil and pad and set up two columns. Label the left-hand side "What I Want," the other side "What They Want." Filling in this list will define your negotiation perimeters. At the top of each column, write down the price —theirs and yours. Then move down the left-hand side. You want them to pay title insurance and any and all repairs you know are needed prior to the sale. Next, look at their side and try to analyze what they want.

Now you can evaluate what you may have to give up for that $8,000 spread. You or someone you know may be a talented carpenter or electrician, in which case you may be able to make the repairs yourself. You may want to pick up the escrow costs (they probably will amount to only $350); perhaps the title insurance costs as well, which, through negotiation, may be picked up for free, or for less than $100. A careful, itemized breakdown of these costs (part of doing your homework) will enable you to enter into the negotiations with confidence.

Don't give them your cost total, ever, ever. Just reel off in your own good time what you are prepared to do. There are many, many variables in a real estate deal. You may find that they're interested in a quick escrow (30 days or sooner) or a slow escrow (three to six months). You will want to take that into consideration. If they want a 90-day escrow, which is extremely fast, you may want to tell them that in exchange for the $8,000 you will be able to move that quickly. Pay particular attention to their response to your query: "How fast do you want to move?" How desperate are they? How *not* desperate are they? Does it appear as though there are other buyers in the picture? This is, of course, an extremely important point.

Rehearsal for the drama of negotiation is also highly advisable. Bargaining is the country cousin of the theatrical arts. You should work up a scenario well in advance, a game plan embracing introductory gambits, diversionary suggestions, counterproposals, crucial arguments, and final position. If you don't, you'll be like an actor who hasn't learned his lines—and you'll feel every bit as foolish. Role-playing is a big help. Days before you enter into negotiation you may undergo intellectual and emotional conditioning by having an associate play the part of your adversary in as hardheaded a manner as you can expect from your opposite numbers at the bargaining table. This can "psych you up" for the session. And it is fun to be psychologically honed for the forthcoming big game.

When I say that negotiating is a form of theater, I mean that a certain amount of thespian ability is extremely helpful. So is a poker face. Pretended disinterest in an adversary's proposal, while you cite possible alternatives to his suggestions, is likely to provide you with an advantage: It will put him on the defensive, in the position of selling *you*—even if secretly you are quite willing to be sold on his proposition.

You'll find that one of the most effective bargaining weapons is silence. Nothing unnerves an adversary so much as an impassive, inscrutable, unresponsive exterior. Here you must school yourself rigorously. You may, while negotiating, find the temptation to fill the silences almost irresistible. Resist, nonetheless. A highly successful real estate broker told me she lost out on a very big piece of industrial property early in her career because, in the face of her adversaries' stolid silence and her own nervousness, she gave away too much.

A display of controlled anger can also be effective if it is used in very special circumstances with people who might be impressed by it. But don't overdo it. If you start raging, you may find yourself with no alternative to stalking out of the bargaining session.

There are several vital don'ts connected with the art of negotiation:

1. Don't assume the other party has the same motivations you do. Everyone comes to a negotiation with a different set of objectives and needs. Your job is to define as quickly as possible your needs *and* the other side's needs.

2. Don't drag a lawyer along until you need one. Lawyers cost lots of money. Recently, in preparation for a meeting, I had a brief conference with an attorney to go over what I should do in case the deal should seem ready to wrap up. I spent a short, solid thirty minutes with him, took extensive notes on his advice, and felt armed with enough to get through the meeting. (And I made sure I knew where and how to get in touch with him if I needed him during the negotiations.)

The presence of legal eagles tends to scare everybody. If you bring a lawyer, the other side will quite naturally want to bring one, too. This can often eliminate any of the necessary, casual give-and-take. People are prone to become unduly formal, even inflexible, in the company of lawyers. As an associate put it once: "Lawyers are often more interested in making things legal than in making the deal." Which is as it should be—things *should* be legal. But there's a time and place for everything, and in early stages of negotiation the bargaining should take priority.

3. Don't neglect the ploy, if you have an associate with you during a bargaining session, of excusing yourself from the meeting in order to discuss strategy. It's perfectly all right to say that you want to discuss with your partner a few points outside the conference room. Simply excuse yourself, take a walk in the hallway, or go out for a cup of coffee, having informed the other side that you'll be back in fifteen minutes. If your opposite number gets hot about it and say, "Abso-

lutely not," be ready to reply: "All right. But in that case you must understand that we won't be able to give you a quick answer."

There is great leverage in this tactic, if used wisely. Such a maneuver can bemuse the opposition. But you should *never* use it if by doing so you appear indecisive or confused. Then you will lose far more than you can hope to gain.

4. Don't agree too quickly. "Bargains made in speed are commonly repented at leisure"—a wise rule of thumb. Don't let yourself be hurried unduly; think the deal through with slow and measured care. Turn it this way and that in your mind before you move. But once you've given your word, stick to it. There is nothing that will destroy your standing more roundly than a reputation for reneging on a deal. Don't.

5. Don't be afraid to walk out, if a crucial point is at issue, or if tempers are getting frayed. (It's preferable to getting into a shouting match.) If the other side doesn't call you back, you can always return anyway. And if you *are* called back, that's usually a sign that the opposition is weakening.

6. If possible, never go into a negotiation unless you're in top shape, physically and mentally; never when you're upset, sad, or sick. I once found myself on the beneficial side of the situation. I was in Kansas City, negotiating a contract for an exclusive distribution agreement for a product. The other party had just undergone oral surgery and was in tremendous pain. I naturally felt very sympathetic, but the upshot of it was that the final agreement turned out to be extraordinarily advantageous for me. There's the other side of the coin, of course. On another occasion, I went into a meeting having just negotiated a large contract, and I was feeling euphoric about it. I ended up giving far too much away simply because I was feeling so good. Remember: The deal you negotiate today, whether it involves real estate, a raise, a new car, or a million-dollar contract, you will have to live with from that point onward. So be sure you go into the match in top form, at the peak of your capabilities, and able to tell yourself that you've done the very best job you could.

7. Finally, never, *never* assume that the other party isn't as intelligent or able as you are. More disasters arise from underestimating the capacities of one's opponent than from any other single mistake. The shock engendered from a miscalculation of this sort will place you at a disadvantage from which you won't easily recover.

A fascinating example of negotiation was conducted by Ruth Houghton Axe, whose meteoric career I've mentioned earlier. Her firm held the balance of power in a proxy fight over the control of a cement company. Axe-Houghton's influence would be decisive in determining whether the long-entrenched old guard would prevail or a group of aggressive young executives would take over. Ruth called a showdown meeting with the two embattled factions. The spokesman for the old guard delivered a smooth and convincing recital of the company's past accomplishments. Ruth interrupted him, saying she hadn't called this meeting to listen to a parade of flowery reminiscences. What concrete plans did he offer now, for the future? The urbane gentleman gave way in some confusion.

The leader of the Young Turks then rose and announced some rather grandiose plans for the future development of the firm. Ruth cut him short too, telling him she wasn't particularly charmed by fanciful promises; what she wanted were solidly outlined and soberly presented programs capable of realization. Both factions retired, neither of them sure where they stood with Ruth Axe, and depressingly aware that they hadn't made much impact with their presentations.

After a brief discussion of the issues, Ruth called on a senior member of the board of directors, who spoke favorably of the incumbent management as gentlemen of the old school, socially acceptable, a credit to the industry, and so on. Next she turned to one of her advisers, who agreed that the Young Turks were uncouth, but argued that they were nevertheless "hungry"—they possessed the requisite ambition and drive to provide the company with the go-go spirit it needed to compete successfully with its rivals. Ruth now turned back to the director, who admitted that this was true and withdrew his former argument.

Probably Ruth had known all along, from her intensive study of the cement company's balance sheets and personnel, that the firm was suffering from tired blood in the upper executive echelons, and that she would come down on the side of the younger men. She perhaps could have predicted what her director would say, and what position her adviser would take. But her *main* objective here was corporate unanimity of view on her own ship; that, and an image of judicial impartiality—and toughness!—with a troubled company with which Axe-Houghton would continue to work. (You can bet those Young Turks quickly came up with some solid, practical programs.) As one associate said, she simply wanted to leave the impression that she was hearing out both sides in a spirit of democratic inquiry. But the meeting achieved a lot more than that.

Whether you're buying or selling, you should always be the salesman in negotiating. Even if you're buying, you have to sell the seller on the idea that he's doing the right thing. This is particularly important if you're buying, for instance, a family business, in which case the idea of continuity is important. You have to persuade the seller that you're worthy of maintaining his family's business.

Remember, the cornerstone of all good negotiation is preparation. That is what will give you flexibility and poise. Essentially, negotiation is simply a matter of trying whatever you want to try. And it is also a matter of practice. Finally, it is a matter of understanding the other person's position as clearly as you do your own. That's the name of the bargaining game.

10 /

Beginning Your Investment Career

At this point, whether you're pursuing a career in a corporation, are interested in improving your financial picture, or have opted for establishing your own business, you are likely to enter the investment world. You've got your financial affairs in order; you've laid part of your financial foundation through savings. Now you need to move ahead confidently.

The purpose of investing is simple. First of all, it's a way of allowing your money to make more money. In other words, to let the money you worked for start working for *you*. Second, if you don't invest your money in some fashion or other it's going to be eroded by inflation. Inflation is not just a contemporary phenomenon; it has existed through the centuries. The difference is that when it stands at a controllable 2 percent or 3 percent, the possibilities for achieving more than that interest rate (and thereby holding your financial gains) is often quite good. But when inflation reaches 5 percent, or higher—much higher, as now—it becomes a major factor not only for the rich but especially for the low- and middle-income brackets.

To give you a specific instance: Let's say you have $100 and you bury it in a tin box in your garden. At the end of one 12-month cycle, if inflation is running at 10 percent, you will be able to buy goods worth only $90 with that original C-note. Here's another way of looking at it: Without investing, you're taking a 10 percent pay cut—instead of your $10,000-a-year salary, you've got to accept $9,000. This is in effect what you're doing if you decide to stay out of the investment field. Your economic survival (certainly your surviving in style) depends on keeping pace with our inflationary patterns.

Your first concern is to acquire the necessary knowledge and expertise to deal confidently in the investment market. There are several ways to do this, but don't delude yourself —once again, there are no easy shortcuts. Nor is there any effective substitute for actual experience.

As I have said, financial seminars are being conducted in increasing numbers by community colleges and universities, by women's groups and banks. These allow you to take advantage of the experience of other women who have mastered the same problems that confront you. In the give-and-take of such sessions you'll learn what sort of investment possibilities are best suited to you. In addition, you may enjoy a shared feeling that yours need not be an isolated effort to find security. Making money is often a joy simply because of the able and engaging people you meet who are intent on the same quest.

Another way to gain expertise is to seek out a professional. Many women have approached me, both at seminars and in casual conversation, and told me: "Oh, yes. I must learn more about finance, but I think the *real* solution for me is to get a financial adviser." Such a comment reveals a very naive attitude about the investment world (similar to mine in the early days). Why? Because financial advisers are simply not interested in someone who has a modest amount of money. By "modest" I mean less than $100,000. Most financial advisers are interested in very large portfolios, thinking that's the only way *they* can make money. And the fact is that the average woman simply is not in those leagues. If you have $250,000 to invest, you can command the attention of a competent financial adviser. But even if you have that much money, the chances are that your portfolio still won't get the kind of tender loving care it needs. The fact is that portfolios are generally run together with other portfolios to reduce the amount of time the adviser must spend on them to make the same amount of money from you—and more money from other investors whose portfolios he has time to handle.

This is not to knock the financial adviser. I've stressed earlier how important it is for you to seek out the professionals in every area—lawyers, bankers, tax accountants—and the financial adviser also has his place. But if you have sufficient funds to engage a good one, you must also bear in mind that while he will take a lot of the responsibility off your shoulders (which means, incidentally, that you'll be losing some of your independence, your right to make your own mistakes and profit from them), you will still need to be virtually as knowledgeable as he is in order to comprehend and evaluate his recommendations.

Nowhere is advice more plentiful than in the investment field. You'll soon become aware of the wide variety of people eager to handle your money and take their slice off the top. Many stockbrokers offer their information free of charge in hope of handling your transactions. There are many financial newsletters and advisory services to which you can subscribe, most of them charging rather heavily for their services; the more successful they've been, presumably, the more they charge for their weekly, monthly, or quarterly bulletins. Your morning paper's financial pages probably offer an enormous range of investment possibilities. On the fringes of all that more or less professional counseling, you'll also find a horde of tipsters—friends, relatives, chance acquaintances—who are eager to tout a stock or other investment. I have learned, the expensive way, to deal only with established firms in the financial area.

"Hot tips" are something to beware of. Usually this "inside information" involves a tantalizing rumor that the stock is about to be split, or a merger is in the offing, or the company behind the stock is going to make a dramatic announcement in the next week or two—a technological breakthrough has been achieved and a product certain to sweep the marketplace is about to be introduced.

Usually this inside information is pure malarkey. If your tipster knows about it, a lot of other people presumably know too; in which case the stock would already have risen sharply. I should also add that there is the little matter of a Securities and Exchange Commission regulation that carries a fine of something around $1,000 if you are caught giving inside corporate information—or if you are the recipient of such inside information and act on it. Forget them. Tips on stock are about as reliable as those offered you by some Damon Runyon character at a racetrack.

The first thing you should remember in embarking on investments, however exciting it is to build independence through a venturesome course of action, is that nothing is sure-fire. No particular form of investment is advisable for everyone. You can afford to be adventurous or conservative in direct proportion to your situation, your responsibilities, your age and prospects—and the amount of money you have to risk.

That's the first thing to consider: a secure base. Whatever your circumstances, you'll need to have a certain amount of your money in a liquid form, readily available in savings accounts or savings and loan deposits. Most experts feel you should have at least $2,000 in savings before considering any investment possibilities. In these days of inflation and uncertainty, $5,000 is probably a more realistic figure. Another rule of thumb is to keep in savings an amount equal to five times your monthly salary.

As soon as you are satisfied that you have provided for a minimum basic savings account, you should turn your attention to the important subject of insurance. Insurance can be grouped into three areas: the group insurance many employers provide, life insurance, and property and casualty insurance. By all means take all the group insurance to which your employment entitles you. Always a good buy, it provides excellent protection in case of accident or the ruinous costs of prolonged illness.

When it comes to property and casualty insurance, your life style will dictate your needs. Whether you own your own house or live in an apartment, you should have a "home-owner's policy," which insures you against the basic risks: fire, burglary, and liability (should someone trip on your living-room rug). These policies are generally written over a three-year term and can be paid in annual installments.

The subject of life insurance is much more complex. Most life insurance policies contain an insurance element *and* an investment element. The easiest way to visualize this is to cite an example: If today you buy a $10,000 whole life insurance policy and your days are ended tomorrow by a Mack truck, your dependents will immediately get a $10,000 payment. This illustrates the pure insurance feature of such a policy.

If, on the other hand, you take out the same policy and live happily for the next 45 years, you will *not* have taken advantage of the insurance feature. Instead, your policy will have amassed a very interesting nest egg for you in the form of its cash value, which will have grown to a respectable size by that time. If the policy continues in force, it will eventually pay off from an insurance viewpoint as well, when you are finally laid to rest.

The great advantage of purchasing life insurance with such an investment feature is the fact that, unlike other investments, you do not actively buy and sell during your lifetime. You make one purchase and then essentially forget about it, simply paying your annual premiums. This protects you from yourself—it allows the cash value to accumulate without your being able to spend it, to invest it foolishly, or otherwise to fritter it away. This psychological "forced" investment feature of life insurance is often its most attractive feature, since the effective interest rate the investment pays is quite poor compared to many other investment alternatives.

The purest form of life insurance, recommended by many experts, is term insurance (apart from group insurance, which normally contains term life). Here you are buying only insurance and will receive no cash value accretions whatever. For those on a very tight budget or those who want to buy maximum life insurance and not mix it up with investment dollars, this is the policy to buy. It will allow you to buy the maximum amount of insurance for the minimum number of premium dollars.

There are all kinds of gradations of life insurance, from term insurance to endowment plans, plans in which you pay premiums only for a limited number of years, and so on. Discuss these with an unbiased professional before committing to one of them.

How much life insurance should you buy? If you are the breadwinner on whom your dependents are totally dependent, a good rule of thumb is to cover your present debts, including the mortgage on your house, if any, and provide for three to five years' income on top of that. Be careful of buying so much insurance that you become "insurance poor," which means that you have no funds left over for other kinds of savings and investments. On the other hand, you should have enough so that if disaster should strike, those who look to you for their support will have an adequate period of transition to provide for their needs.

If your circumstances dictate a conservative attitude toward investment, you should consider alternatives to the high-risk possibilities of the stock market and the more sophisticated forms of multiplying your assets. The higher your potential return on any investment, the greater the risk. Only you can determine, after acquiring a basic knowledge of your investment options, just how much risk you can afford to take.

In addressing seminars organized to help women understand that marketplace, I always point out that there are three things you can do with your money: hold it in cash, loan it out for income, or make it appreciate in value. Between the first and third of those alternatives there is all the difference between a tricycle and a racing car.

To illustrate what I mean, here's a ten-second quiz for you.

Which would you rather have: $50,000, or the figure arrived at by taking one cent and doubling it every day for thirty days? Don't hesitate, now. You'd take the $50,000? You've been fooled, and royally: The sum that you're passing up is $5,368,709.12!

There's a simple rule of thumb often cited by investment experts, called the Rule of 72. It says that to find how many years it takes your money to double, just divide 72 by the annual interest rate. If you loan money at 4 percent, it takes 18 years to double. If you invest at 12 percent growth, it takes only six years.

Back to inflation for a moment. It's a topic that's been done to death of late, and I'm not going to bore you with a lot of doom-and-gloom statistics. Inflation is here, it's going to be with us awhile longer; it's actually been with us for at least the past forty years. The difference lies in the fact that formerly it was running at that negligible rate of 2 to 3 percent a year; today, inflation has reached 11 percent in the United States, 26 percent in Japan, and up into the 100s in South America.

Actually, as I like to say in seminars, there's a plus side to this distressing business of inflation. I'm not playing Pollyanna here. What's happened is that inflation has made discussion about money (or the lack of it) fashionable. Everyone, from the very rich to low-income groups, is suddenly talking about money: how to make it, how to conserve it, how to beat inflation with it. It's fashionable too, these days, to know what the prime rate is; as little as twelve months ago, few people knew of the existence of the Federal Reserve, let alone its function in our monetary system. Sex may have been the hot topic of the sixties, but money is definitely the compelling subject of the seventies. And this is all to the good, because inflation is not in itself the kind of thing you or I can do anything about; inflation and the economy in general are in the hands of the government and the bankers. We can, however, learn to function profitably within the situation. And it is here that investments should loom large in your thinking.

Think of yourself, for the moment, as being on a vast conveyor belt that is sliding backwards at 11 miles an hour. You're driving a little car on the belt—one of these little golf carts, say—and it's capable of five and occasionally six or seven miles per hour. You're moving, but in the wrong direction. You're being carried back and back, and eventually you're going to fall off the end of the belt.

That's exactly what your savings account is doing: Its annual yield of 5½ percent simply cannot keep up with our double-digit inflation. Even the time deposit accounts (see page 129) give you only roughly 8 percent, and you're subject to severe penalities if you withdraw prematurely. What you need, obviously, is a pattern of investment that will get you up in the 10 to 12 percent range—one in which the value of your capital has a chance of appreciating still further. That way, you stay ahead of the game—or at least even.

This is not to declare savings accounts to be worthless. While not an aggressive investment, they have their place. They should comprise an important part of everyone's financial foundation.

If you are self-employed or if your employer does not have a "qualified" pension, retirement, or profit-sharing plan, the tax law provides two ways in which you can create a retirement plan of your own. If you are self-employed, the so-called Keogh plan allows you to set aside up to $7,500 a year in special forms of banks or savings and loan accounts, securities, or an "open end" mutual fund. If you are employed and your employer does not have a qualified retirement plan, you can set aside up to $1,500 but not more than 15 percent of your salary in the same fashion. In each case, these amounts are directly tax deductible by you whether you itemize your deductions or not. And you pay taxes neither on these contributions nor on the income they in turn earn over the years until you are retired, at which time presumably you are in a lower tax bracket than at present. Check with your banker, accountant, insurance agent, or stockbroker about the specific details of the investments qualified for these retirement plans.

What you should aim for (depending, of course, on your own particular circumstances) is a careful balance of low-income, low-risk assets and more aggressive, high-risk holdings. The following is a diagram of a financial planning pyramid I show at seminars, to demonstrate as graphically as possible the comparative risks and opportunities associated with the various forms of investment:

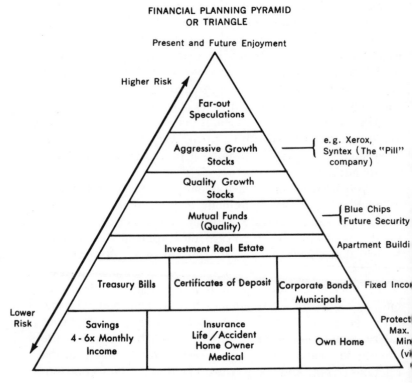

FINANCIAL PLANNING PYRAMID
OR TRIANGLE

For those of you who have to be cautious in an investment program, the following, on a rising scale of risk, are some of the opportunities available.

A *standard bank savings account.* Low interest, very low risk.

Long-term (time deposit) or investment savings accounts. These pay a higher rate of interest but commit you to leaving your money on deposit for a certain period, usually one to four years. If you have to withdraw before the term is up, you pay a severe penalty. So you'd better be certain you can afford to have your money tied up over that length of time.

U.S. savings bonds. Low interest, but high degree of security, because they are direct obligations of the federal government. Their advantage is primarily psychological. To obtain the normal interest, you have to hold on to them for five years. If you cash them in during the early years, you get very little interest. The bulk of the interest builds up in the last years of the bond's life, thus tending to force you to keep them until maturity. They can be purchased in small denominations, starting at $25. They can be bought through any bank or through your company's payroll deduction plan.

Treasury bills. These, too, offer a high degree of security. They are sold in minimum amounts of $10,000, with interest often higher than savings accounts. Interest rates of Treasury bills have varied from around 2 percent to over 8 percent. These rates are set on the basis of an auction held each Monday, and therefore change continually in broad up-and-down movements in rhythm with general short-term interest rate levels. They mature in three, six or twelve months.They can be purchased for a nominal fee through banks or through stock-brokerages, or without a fee directly from the nearest of the thirteen Federal Reserve banks.

Treasury bonds. These are longer-term obligations of the U.S. Treasury and are also sold in $1,000 minimums. Their life is up to thirty years. If you wish to buy Treasury bonds already issued and outstanding, you can pick the number of remaining years of life depending on your inclination, and the effective yield will vary with the number of years remaining. As with all publicly traded bonds, the major risk you incur (other than inflation) is the possibility that you may have to sell the bonds before their maturity date, at which time they may be selling for substantially less than your cost, if prevailing long-term interest rates are then very high. In other words, their yield varies as does that of other bonds on the basis of long-term interest rates.

Government agency bonds. These are issued by such governmental institutions as the Federal Land Bank. They pay high interest rates (typically ½ percent higher than U.S. Treasury bonds); they also carry a higher risk, since they are not direct government obligations.

Certificates of deposit. These are short-term IOUs issued by commercial banks normally up to one year. Rates therefore vary from bank to bank. It is important to know that the interest rates on CDs over $100,000 are not fixed by the government; however, they are regulated for amounts under $100,000. Therefore, in periods of high interest rates their interest rates greatly exceed interest paid on ordinary accounts. They are purchased through the individual bank and the interest rate varies with the amount. A smaller interest rate is paid for a $10,000 CD and a higher interest rate is paid for a $100,000 CD.

Commercial paper. Large corporations such as General Motors Acceptance Corporation, Sears, Roebuck, and Montgomery Ward frequently issue so-called commercial paper to cover their own short-term financial needs. Commercial paper is simply a corporation's note or IOU agreeing to pay back the amount borrowed from the public in one to six months at a specified interest rate. Commercial paper is usually purchased through a commercial bank, has a $10,000 minimum investment, and typically pays approximately 1 percent more than Treasury bills. The notes are backed by the credit of the issuing company, which is normally a very large, stable organization.

With private companies issuing commercial paper, as with government agencies, a note or bond is given the investor. In effect, it's an IOU that states that between date of issue and maturity date they will pay you a certain amount of interest on, say, the thousand dollars you have lent them. Your security lies in the credit and stability of the issuing company or agency. You always run the risk, of course, that these obligations will not be met. If you should have to liquidate the holdings before they mature, there is a market for such notes and bonds, access to which is available through bankers and stockbrokers.

I have cited the above possibilities for the benefit of those who cannot afford to run the risk of dealing with what I call "aggressive money." Every investor, however, should always keep a certain percentage of her resources in the bottom blocks of the pyramid.

Many ambitious and successful career women, including myself, have been able to take a more venturesome course—as much through luck and circumstance, I hasten to add, as through any extraordinary virtue. Our comparative youth, money we have earned in high-salaried jobs or acquired through inheritance, independence of family responsibilities—factors like these have freed many of us of the necessity to consider safety above potential reward. Succeeding chapters, accordingly, will deal with the opportunities open to those who can afford to be aggressive in the money markets.

Before you plunge into them, having educated youself to some degree, you'll realize that, as in any educational process, you have to pay your tuition. Experimentation, like breakage in a school laboratory, can be costly. Unless you're unusually wary or lucky, your "tuition" will be paid in the form of occasionally losing money.

With that caution in mind, you should proceed to another area of knowledge before making any sizable forays in the investment field. How do you know which company is worthy of investment? And how do you find out the true condition of the company behind the stock that has attracted your interest?

The only way to find the answer to such a crucial question is by learning to read—or decipher—a company's annual financial report. You can get a company's annual report by writing or telephoning the corporate office directly, or your stockbroker can get it for you. Most companies are happy to send out their annual reports to potential investors. Unfortunately, to most of us such reports are an almost trackless swamp of statistics and corporate prose.

The long-established brokerage firm of Merrill Lynch, Pierce, Fenner and Smith, in an excellent pamphlet issued for prospective investors, has some wise words on the necessity of mastering this admittedly difficult but essential subject:

All annual reports bring their readers written messages whose rhetoric ranges from stodgy to mod, from murky to magnificently clear. The purpose of these messages, signed or unsigned, is to put the best possible face on whatever has happened to the corporation during the year. There is nothing wrong in this, for optimism is no less a virtue in corporate executives than in generals.

Most annual reports will delight you with exquisite pictures of plants and products, people and places. . . . More and more, annual reports are becoming lavish exercises in printing and publishing. This, too, is fine, so long as costs don't deprive stockholders of too much of their dividends. Since large corporations as a general rule must publish annual reports, then why not make those annual reports as pretty as possible as well as kind to the corporate management which put them out?

The Merrill Lynch brochure urges you to enjoy the elegant prose and the imaginative typography of the annual report —and then to turn a cold and critical eye to the balance sheet that accompanies the fine writing.

You cannot miss it, for the balance sheet is the formidable section of numbers that somehow wind up all even—as though the whole corporation balanced precariously in some sort of mathematical scales. Its language may be thorny and its rows of figures seem as impenetrable as anything else in your annual report, but the balance sheet holds the key to your journey out of the jungle and into the cultivated country of facts.

The main thing is not to panic and let all that fine print turn into an impenetrable blur. The thorny part of reading and evaluating a balance sheet is the specialized language of the accountants who draw it up. Once you decipher that code, you can readily grasp what it conveys of a company's status.

As you can see the balance sheet is divided into two parallel sections: on the left the assets, on the right the liabilities and stockholders' equity in the company. Under "Assets" are listed everything the company owns—plant, equipment, goods, and property—plus uncollected claims against other companies. Under "Liabilities" you see the details of the company's indebtedness, plus the total invested by its stockholders.

Here's the way the breakdown for a typical company goes:

Assets will include cash, both in the company treasury and in its bank accounts. Marketable securities in which the company's excess or idle cash has been invested are also included—usually listed at the price paid for them, with current market value in parentheses. Under "Accounts receivable" will be found the total owed the company on products shipped to customers who are expected to pay up in 30, 60, or 90 days; against that is set a stated sum, the bad debt reserve, which is supposed to offset any accounts receivable that are defaulted. The left-hand side of the balance sheet also lists the total of the company's inventories of raw materials, goods in the process of being manufactured, and finished goods awaiting shipment.

Also itemized on the balance sheet are "fixed assets": the property occupied by the company, its plant and manufacturing equipment, office furniture and equipment, and any forms of transport owned by the company. These are valued at

NATIONAL ELECTRIC CORPORATION

BALANCE SHEET—JUNE 30, 1975

	1975	1974
ASSETS		
Current Assets		
Cash	$ 450,000	$ 300,000
Marketable securities at cost (market value: 1975, $890,000; 1974, $480,000)	850,000	460,000
Accounts receivable *Less:* allowance for bad debt: 1975, $100,000; 1974, $95,000	2,000,000	1,900,000
Inventories	2,700,000	3,000,000
Total current assets	**$6,000,000**	$5,660,000
Fixed assets		
Land	$ 450,000	$ 450,000
Building	3,800,000	3,600,000
Machinery	950,000	850,000
Office equipment	100,000	95,000
	$5,300,000	$4,995,000
Less: accumulated depreciation	**1,800,000**	1,500,000
Net fixed assets	**$3,500,000**	$3,495,000
Prepayments and deferred charges	100,000	90,000
Intangibles (goodwill, patent, trademarks)	100,000	100,000
Total assets	**$9,700,000**	$9,345,000

LIABILITIES	1975	1974
Current liabilities		
Accounts payable	$1,000,000	940,000
Notes payable	850,000	1,000,000
Accrued expenses payable	330,000	300,000
Federal income taxes payable	320,000	290,000
Total current liabilities	$2,500,000	$2,530,000
Long-term liabilities		
First mortgage bonds; 5% interest, due 1985	2,700,000	2,700,000
Total liabilities		
	$5,200,000	$5,230,000

STOCKHOLDERS' EQUITY

Capital stock

Preferred stock, 5% cumulative, $100 par value each; authorized, issued, and outstanding 6,000 shares	600,000	600,000
Common stock, $5 par value each; authorized, issued, and outstanding 300,000 shares	1,500,000	1,500,000
Capital surplus	700,000	700,000
Accumulated retained earnings	1,700,000	1,315,000
Total stockholders' equity	$4,500,000	$4,115,000
Total liabilities and stockholders' equity	$9,700,000	$9,345,000

cost, minus the depreciation estimated to have occurred as of the date of the balance sheet. Listed as assets, too, are "pre-payments." For example, the company may have paid up fire insurance for the three-year period of its premium, or paid rental in advance on leased or rented equipment.

Liabilities will include, first, all debts that will fall due during the coming year. Accountants will tell you that the relationship between "current assets" and "current liabilities" is a key factor in analyzing a balance sheet. Into this category fall accounts payable—the total the company owes its creditors; notes payable, the amount owed to banks and other lending sources. Another item under this heading is "accrued expenses payable," which is the money the company owes on a given day in wages paid its employees, interest on loans, attorneys' fees, insurance premiums, pensions, and the taxes due the Internal Revenue Service. Then there are long-term liabilities, all debts due after one year from the date of the balance sheet. Also on that side of the balance sheet is listed all the capital stock, preferred and common, and the paid-in capital (the total paid by shareholders over the par or legal value of each share).

Several other items on the balance sheet should command your attention.

One is "accumulated retained earnings," sometimes called "earned surplus." This amount represents earnings above the dividends the company has paid out. It's a good idea to compare this figure with those of prior years. A steady growth in retained earnings means the corporation is becoming financially stronger. Most annual reports contain a ten-year summary of the financial data, so that the most up-to-date report can give you all the information you need about prior years.

Something else to watch is the "net working capital" figure, the difference between total current assets and total current liabilities. If there is a considerable margin, this too is an indication of financial strength. According to financial analysts, *current assets should ideally be two to one over current liabilities.*

You should also check the figures showing the turnover in inventory. Inventory turnover is defined as cost of sales divided by the latest inventory figure on the balance sheet. This ratio tells you how many times per year the company's inventory is turned over or sold. A cost of sales to inventory ratio of 2:1 is quite low, one of 10:1 quite high. This will, of course, vary greatly from industry to industry and company to company. And the sales figures for the current year should be compared with those of several previous years. Two questions to ask on this score: Have sales steadily risen? Did the company preserve a comfortable profit margin on the increased business?

The price-earnings ratio, for many investors, is of primary importance. Remember, this is calculated by dividing the market price of the stock by the earnings per share. If the stock is selling at $25 a share and earning $2 a share, the price-earnings ratio is 12½ to 1. The stock is thus said to be selling at 12½ times earnings. If the stock rose to 40, that ratio would rise to 20. A company with solid growth will probably double its earnings every five to seven years. But a decline in the price-earnings ratio is usually a cautionary signal. During the boom of the sixties the price-earnings ratios of some glamour issues rose to 60 and 100, but they dropped considerably during the gloomier seventies.

Merrill Lynch's brochure advises prospective investors to examine carefully the footnotes appended to the balance sheet, possibly including such items as changes in method of depreciating fixed assets, and contingent liabilities listing claims or pending lawsuits against the company.

You're not through yet, for the balance sheet is only one of the statements you will find in an annual report. As you have probably noticed, the balance sheet shows only the fundamental soundness of the company, but not how much money it is presently making—and without that information it's like a television set without a picture. The picture in this case is the income statement, also commonly called (for confusion's sake) a profit and loss statement, "P&L," as well as an earnings report.

By whatever name, its basic purpose is to show the operating activities of a company for an entire year so you can compare it with previous years' results. This comparison will give you some insight into whether the company is moving ahead, standing still or losing ground.

NATIONAL ELECTRIC CORPORATION

INCOME STATEMENT	1975	1974
Net sales	$11,000,000	$10,200,000
Cost of sales	8,500,000	7,959,000
Selling & general expense	1,400,000	1,325,000
Income from operations	$ 1,100,000	$ 916,000
Less: Interest expense	(135,000)	(135,000)
Other income and expenses	50,000	27,000
Income before federal income taxes	1,015,000	808,000
Income taxes	480,000	365,000
Net income	$ 535,000	$ 443,000

The way this is done is to match the income of a company against all the costs (and expenses) required to run it. The result at the end of the year is net income or, sadly, a net loss.

Our sample income statement for our old standby, National Electric (which is like that of most other companies) has Net sales as the first category. That is the total amount of money the company has received from customers for its goods sold or services rendered (less returned goods, allowances and discounts).

Next, we have Cost of sales, which means all the costs incurred in the factory that go into making the product. That would be raw materials plus labor (people) and include such items as rent, electricity, supplies, maintenance and repairs.

The next item, Selling and general expense, includes two categories. Selling expense is the dollars used in selling the product to the customer; it includes the salaries of the people in the sales department, their travel, and associated office expense. General expense includes all the money spent for the "front office" *other* than the sales department, and that portion of the general office expense not specifically allocated to selling or the factory.

Then we get to Income from operations, which is arrived at by the simple process of subtracting the Costs and expenses from the Net sales figure.

Any interest expense for money the company has borrowed would appear on the next line—Interest expense.

Next is the line where income to the company other than through the sale of its product is shown. A typical example would be dividends and interest the company earns through its investments in stocks and bonds.

The total of all the above gives us Income before taxes, and the rest of the statement is self-explanatory. The famous "bottom line" is Net income.

Analysts are particularly urgent in suggesting that you compare several years' results to obtain a clear picture of the company's progress or retrogression. A long backward view will show:

1. The trend of sales fluctuations.

2. The trend of earnings as compared to sales.

3. The company's reaction to general trends in the national economy.

4. The increase or decrease in return on capital.

5. Net earnings per share of common stock.

6. The company's continuing policy on dividends, whether it tends to increase such payments in ratio to increased earnings or prefers to plow the money back into the corporation as a whole.

The experts emphasize that financial statements have only

half the value they should if they are "studied in a vacuum"—that is, without comparing them to those of previous years. They are your surest guide to investment. Once you've mastered the art of reading and analyzing them, you'll be on your way to an aggressive investment program.

11 /

Your Safari into
the Investment Jungle

From what you have read about Wall Street, you may well have imagined it a jungle, populated by legendary beasts who take a special delight in gobbling up widows, divorcees, and housewives innocent of the beast's dietary preferences. Well, Wall Street *is* a place to tread warily, with your eyes open and your senses alert—just like any marketplace where the stakes are high. Other observers, no more knowledgeable, like to compare the financial districts with Las Vegas casinos. But there is more law and regulation governing Wall Street and its tributaries than any gambling den, and the more you know about the investment world, the safer you are.

The facts are that stock market business is your business. The market has been called the backbone of the American free enterprise system; it boasts 33 million investors, and half of those 33 million are *women* investors. One of the reasons for the market's popularity lies in the unique opportunity for betting on the success of American business. Then there is the fact that all investments are liquid—there is usually a ready market at some price for the purchase or sale of your investment. (Stock market adherents often advance this argument for the market as against, say, real estate, which is not nearly so negotiable as a security.) All well and good, but the most powerful attraction the market has for a great many people is excitement.

Study, information-gathering, an acquired ability to analyze on your own, a habit of being practical and objective—all these will serve as your most reliable guides to that exciting world. The more you learn about the subject, the less mysterious and forbidding it becomes.

If possible you should take a personal look at the way Wall Street, or your nearest stock exchange, operates. Some years ago, when I first became interested in the possibilities offered by the financial world, I trekked down to lower Manhattan, made the grand tour of the New York Stock Exchange, and watched the trading activities. It's reassuring to find that the atmosphere is sober, efficient, and businesslike.

It is absolutely vital to scout the territory, study your chosen investment area, and test its feasibility with every means available to you. This doesn't exclude the exercise of good old-fashioned common sense. Shirley Chilton once told me a story that makes this point vividly:

"I'll always remember back in 1956, after I'd been promoted from the switchboard to operations manager and had become a registered representative of this company, how a little old lady kept coming in almost every day, sat near my desk, and kept watching the tape on New York Stock Exchange transactions. She was about eighty years old.

"One day she spoke up. 'Honey,' she told me, 'I want to buy a stock.' I told her I thought it would be important to be sure she had enough money in a bank account and adequate assets before she embarked upon a risk venture.

"But she said, 'I'm eighty years old, honey. I've been around. I know what I want and I want to buy Brunswick.'

"Brunswick was a speculative issue, a company that manufactured sporting equipment and built bowling alleys, selling at about seven dollars per share. 'Don't you want to buy something more stable that pays a dividend?' I asked her. She insisted on Brunswick. So I questioned her about her financial situation to determine if she could risk investing in the stock market, decided that she could afford the risk, and had her sign a statement absolving Reeves if her hunch—or whatever it was—turned out disastrously. She said she wanted to buy five hundred shares of Brunswick.

"I asked her why she picked Brunswick, and she told me, 'I often visit the bowling alley with my son. I see an awful lot of people patronizing that place. It's busy day and night, and I can't find a place to sit down. It must be a good growth business, bowling alleys.'

"Now that was a very sensible observation. The bowling alley boom had just begun. Brunswick stock went up and up. When it reached sixty-three, finally, she instructed me to sell it. Again I asked her why she decided that now's the time—the stock was still on the rise. 'Because,' she said, 'when I go to the bowling alley now, I can find a place to sit down.'

"The Brunswick stock did rise higher, about ten points, after she sold it. But she had been wise in making her move when she did. The only time to sell a stock is too soon. That little old lady's success in financial management is something I've never forgotten. It showed me that a woman with common sense and powers of observation can do as well as anyone else, even without long-term expertise."

With a sound and sensible approach, you can find the joy and adventure of operating in your own personal sector of the financial world.

Of course, you don't actually have to go out and buy a stock. You can practice by selecting one from the financial pages of your newspaper, and then follow its progress on a day-to-day basis as though you owned it. That way you can, in effect, go through all the decision-making process and develop a feeling about a stock, watching all news breaks that arise with respect to that particular company—its personnel changes, its expansion, its quarterly earnings reports. While this does not hold the same emotional overtones as actual buying and selling, it's one way (especially for the more cautious) of gaining an educational base in the market.

Let's take a quick look at the Street, as it's called, and how it came about. The American stock market is almost as old as the republic, dating back to congressional authority for an $80 million bond issue to pay part of the costs of the Revolution. Some years later, in 1792, 24 bigwigs stood under a buttonwood tree on Wall Street and signed an agreement for trading stocks; this was the seedling of the New York Stock Exchange, often called the "Big Board." In the middle of the nineteenth century another outdoor market sprang up, called the Curb (that's where its members conducted their business); it later became the American Stock Exchange.

Those first two exchanges—to be followed by more than a dozen others, from Boston to San Francisco—transformed the nature of American finance and industry. Formerly, American businesses and industries had been entirely controlled by the men who invested their private fortunes in them. More and more companies, needing capital to expand with the times, began offering shares of their stock to the public to finance new growth. That's how the American economy came to be owned by millions of people, instead of remaining a tight little oligarchy.

The people who conduct the business of those exchanges, managing the sale and transfer of all those thousands of stocks and hundreds of millions of dollars, are the brokers who buy "seats" on the exchange which cost a small fortune in themselves (more than half a million dollars back in the flush period a few years ago). In addition to the New York and American Stock Exchanges, and those in various other cities, there is the over-the-counter market, which deals in thousands of minor issues, for the most part, whose companies haven't attained the size and profitability to be listed on a major exchange. The name comes from the fact that such issues were once literally traded over the counter of a bank or similar institution. Obviously stocks sold on the OTC market generally represent small companies with an uncertain future; if the companies trading over the counter succeed and grow, and can meet the requirements of an exchange, they advance to the American and then to the Big Board. I'll have more to say about this later.

The frenetic trading sessions of the major stock exchanges,

with their bewildering jargon and tumultuous clamor, needn't concern you directly. If you've educated yourself in the mechanics of the money game and calculated how much money you want to invest, you'll want to know how to enter the marketplace. Obviously you can't dash onto the trading floor of a stock exchange waving a sheaf of currency; that's the prerogative of the professional traders.

So you'll need an intermediary—a stockbroker.

Picking the right broker is an important part of your investment decision-making. A broker who takes an intelligent interest in your financial situation, who will further the process of educating you in the ways of the money world, will make all the difference between a good return on your money and mediocre results. This doesn't mean that you should feel compelled to charm him into taking a personal interest in your problems; accept his role as that of a professional who, incidentally, profits from the relationship.

You should know that many male brokers are a little prejudiced against women clients. Perhaps a woman broker would be more understanding; but when it comes to handling your money, you should pick out the best person available, regardless of sex. You should know that it is not uncommon for male brokers to claim that women investors can be "difficult"—that they tend to be too "emotional," particularly if a stock goes down or they feel they've been given bad advice; that they have been known to "make scenes." Obviously you should do your part in eradicating this impression of the woman investor as a flighty creature given to overreacting. Be calm, sensible, businesslike, and tough-minded. Pin down your broker on the reasons for the advice given you.

Another way of building up mutual respect is to keep your word in all verbal transactions. Male brokers, again, have told me that some women tend to renege. They will tell their broker to buy 100 shares of a certain stock, at the day's market price of $52. Next morning the stock drops to $48. When the confirmation statement arrives from the brokerage, she tells the broker that she distinctly remembers saying that she told him to buy at $46, not $52. Chances are she'll get away with reneging once—but no one will ever act on her oral order again. The brokerage firms are not in the business of paying people money out of their own pockets. They bought that stock at $52 for her account, on her instructions. If she did not accept, the broker was out the $4 difference between purchase price and present market value.

In finding a broker, you should go about the selection process very carefully. Look on it as a kind of marriage. You don't want to get stuck with the wrong kind of partner. If you don't have much money to invest, you may want to select a large firm with many local branch offices geared to the smaller investor, such as Merrill Lynch, E. F. Hutton, Paine Webber, or Bache and Company. But the most important key is the type and size of account your individual broker is handling.

"One way to find a suitable broker," Shirley Chilton told me, "is to ask your friends for someone who has proved satisfactory to them. But don't necessarily take their advice. Go around and talk to the managers of brokerages. Tell yourself: 'I'm going to be very fussy. I'm going to ask penetrating questions. I will seek a range of opinion, just as I would consult more than one doctor if major surgery were recommended to me.'"

She added: "Your prospective broker should ask you pertinent questions, too, to make sure you're in a position to invest in stocks. But *you* should do most of the questioning. Ask such questions as 'What percentage of your clients have made a profit?' and 'Would you please give me the names and telephone numbers of four clients who have made money with you and four who have not?' Very few people use this interview technique in selecting a brokerage to handle their investments, but they should."

Her own philosophy as a broker is forthright and considerate: Service to the customer on a long-term basis is the only feasible aim. "If I'm going to be successful, my customers are going to have to be successful. I will not sell a stock I don't believe in. The first thing to determine about a prospective customer is what degree of risk he or she wants to take. Then I ask myself what I would do in her position."

Before committing yourself to any particular brokerage, it's an excellent idea to get the feel of its operations. A brokerage is partly a public place; a mirror image, in a sense, of the stock market itself. There's a large area with comfortable seats for people who simply want to come in and watch the action on an electronic board that reports the current activity on the major exchanges, the minute-to-minute fluctuations in stock prices. From sensing the atmosphere of the place, from the conversation of people around you (who presumably are clients of the firm), you'll gather an impression of the way it operates. Many of the larger establishments have information officers whose responsibility it is to answer any questions you may have.

When you've finally made up your mind to work with a certain broker, you should be very clear in your mind just how much you want to invest, what kind of stocks you want to buy (blue chip, glamour issues, growth companies), and how long you want to hang on to them if the price undergoes sizable fluctuations.

You must be prepared for the fact that the broker will ask you probing questions about your finances. That's his job, undertaken for mutual protection, and you shouldn't resent the questions. The broker will want to know all about your sources of income, your net worth, what investments you may already have made. He will also want to know how much you want to invest at the moment, and whether you'll want to make continuing investments or if, say, you intend to devote part of your income monthly or quarterly or annually, in uniform sums, to increasing your portfolio.

No doubt he will explain to you—certainly he should explain to you—the important factors in selecting a stock for investment. There's the risk factor: Stock prices obviously fluctuate under the impact of general economic conditions, threat of war or foreign upheaval, changes in the marketplace, political storms (like Watergate or a coming election), the rise and fall of corporate fortunes. The broker probably will also explain to you the dividend factor. Stocks paying high dividends are not usually growth issues, but are fine for long-term investment because they provide you with a steady income.

Many investors, I've found, often encounter difficulty in understanding that AT&T, which pays a solid dividend, isn't considered a growth stock. It was one, of course, during the early sixties, when AT&T's research department was coming up with technological breakthroughs; it lost its growth glamour when the federal government began threatening—and finally, late in 1974, did undertake—antitrust action that may divest AT&T of some of its subsidiaries. Fast-growth stocks, you will probably be informed, don't usually pay high dividends for two reasons: The company needs to retain cash to finance its rapid growth and because shrewd speculators have driven up their prices in relation to their earnings; the hope that a growth company's earnings will greatly increase in the near future justifies a current high price and forecasts still higher prices for its stock.

With your broker's advice you will determine the answers to several questions: Do you want a "safe" stock that will provide a fixed income annually? Do you want to take a chance and buy a stock you believe will rise dramatically but meanwhile will not be paying much in dividends? Or do you want a stock that combines both those qualities, paying a reasonably satisfactory dividend while promising a rise in its market value?

From the suggestions he makes and the advice he gives, you can gather a lot about the broker's fitness to act as your intermediary with the stock market. You shouldn't be overpersuaded if his concepts simply fit in with yours. You may need a more independent view from your broker.

I use the male pronoun for a broker, I should explain, because our sex has barely got its foot in the financial door at the moment. There are 49,000 registered representatives attached to the brokerage firms with membership in the New York Stock Exchange, and less than 2,000 of these are women.

But don't be discouraged by our lack of numbers. Usually, a woman broker *has to be good* or she wouldn't have attained her position, and she *is* more likely to be sympathetic to another woman's problems.

Take the rather spectacular career of Louise Phipps Hart, who found herself a divorcee twelve years ago with three children to raise—"no assets, no house, no car"—and who, though she had majored in English in college and had no special training for the field, went on to become a $50,000-a-year stockbroker with Shields-Model-Roland, Inc., one of the five foremost block-trading securities firms in the United States (those who sell to large funds and other institutions).

"I chose securities for one key reason," she says. "I could go to work at six in the morning [because of the time difference between Los Angeles and New York, which causes the New York Stock Exchange tickers to come to life at the crack of the California dawn] and get home at three to be with the kids."

Mrs. Hart, who bicycles the fifteen miles to work, makes a point of putting the human equation first. "Some brokers operate on the theory that their time is money; they can't be bothered with little things. I don't work that way. I am infinitely available to my clients, and if they want information, I get it for them. I work long hours, but there is always time to do the things you want to do. A large part of my success is that I have a very loyal clientele, one that refers me to their friends." Obviously Louise Hart, like Shirley Chilton, adds a welcome human touch, warmer and more personal, to what can be a rather cold and impersonal business.

Madelon Talley, at forty-two, is president of the Dreyfus Offshore Trust and manages portfolios worth more than $60 million. It's a tremendous responsibility, but she is stimulated, she says, by the opportunity to "run aggressive money"—a phrase I happen to admire and often quote, because it suggests the venturesome spirit you need to acquire financial independence. And there's Muriel Siebert, the first woman to assume the presidency of a major brokerage and the first woman ever elected to a seat on the New York Stock Exchange (a privilege that, incidentally, cost her $445,000).

"My sudden fame and visibility brought with them great obligations," she recalls. "Not only did I have to prove to my colleagues that I had bought the seat for business reasons, I also had to be a fitting model to all those young women who said, 'You're my ideal; you inspired me.' "

And then, human nature being what it is, there are certain brokerage types you should beware of, whose reputations are often common knowledge.

The worst type is the overactivist. He tries to persuade you to make rapid switches in your holdings. He gets you to buy and sell so often ("churns" your account) that you don't make much money—the profits are leaking away into his commissions on each transaction.

You should also be wary of the kind of broker who offers his suggestions for investment off the top of his head, without seeming to have the necessary research at his fingertips. Good brokers have excellent research depearments to keep them on top of, or ahead of, trends in the market.

Many experts feel that anyone with a considerable amount of money at her disposal should have two brokers handling her affairs. It isn't a good idea to let either know that you are splitting your business, because brokers find repugnant the idea of competing for the attention of one customer. Nevertheless, having two brokers may work to your advantage. You can check on a certain stock with both of them. If both agree it's a good investment, you are doubly reassured. If they disagree, if one says it's very risky, you'll know you should proceed with caution.

A quick but penetrating look at a company is provided by the Standard and Poor sheets available on all major publicly traded companies through your broker. Each sheet is composed of a two-page condensed analysis of the company's primary business, its history, recent trends, and outstanding developments. It contains a chart showing the price history of this company's stock versus its industry and the Dow Jones Industrial Average. In addition, it offers a condensed ten-year summary of pertinent income statement and balance sheet statistics, along with a general recommendation to sell, hold, or buy.

The Standard and Poor sheet can logically be the starting point for the layman's security analysis. From there you can go on to read the company's annual report, the much more detailed and candid 10 K report it has to submit to the Securities and Exchange Commission (available from the SEC), as well as various analysts' industry and company analyses. The regular reading of such financial publications as the *Wall Street Journal, Barron's,* and *Forbes* will lend background and an in-depth feel and sharpen your analytical acumen.

There's another way to further your own private research and development. Let's say that a certain company interests you as an investment possibility. You can ask brokers for their opinion of its potential growth and the probable rise or fall of its stock price. To obtain a more intimate feeling of how the company operates, and who does the operating, I've found the annual stockholders' meeting a valuable source of information and insight.

Supposedly such conclaves are open to stockholders only, but gate-crashing isn't against any civil or corporate laws. I've never heard of anyone's being booted out simply because she didn't own stock in the company. I've attended half a dozen annual meetings of companies in which I held not one share of stock. The only people who have trouble gaining admittance are chronic troublemakers, who get their kicks out of disrupting the proceedings. Some of the troublemakers, those actually owning stock, can't be barred, of course, and they usually enliven the session by badgering the company officers with detailed questions on the company's various activities during the past year. Often they own only a few shares, but can't be prevented from sounding off on the theme that "big corporations are getting away with too much." (And sometimes, like the unabashed heroine of *The Solid Gold Cadillac,* their irreverent queries can have a very healthy corporate effect.)

You'll find that the opening part of the meeting is taken up with a lot of procedures required by law or company regulations—not very interesting after you've heard it a time or two. Then comes the speech by the chairman or president summarizing the year's results, followed by a question-and-answer forum, in which stockholders ask about the company's prospects, possible earnings, new products, sales record, granting of stock options to company officers, directors, and favored employees. And the president and his associates in management have to stand up and account for their corporate decisions, no matter how many gadflies are buzzing about or how idiotic their questions may be. You get a good idea of the management's style, its coolness, its concern for the people who have invested their savings in its future, by the way the brass hats handle themselves in such confrontations. If I observed a company president getting flustered, or displaying unwarranted arrogance, or being unsure of his facts, I'd be very cautious about investing in the corporation.

Another way to familiarize yourself with the possibilities of investment is to pick out a company located in your area. Make yourself an expert on its operations, on the fluctuations of its stock, on any new product line it may be introducing. Proximity in itself can be a big help in deciding on an investment. Let's take a specific case. If you live in the Los Angeles area, you might zero in on an outfit like Occidental Petroleum, which catches my attention at the moment because it has had a spectacular career, growing from practically nothing to a major producer first in Libya and now, possibly, if certain large-scale plans develop, in the Soviet Union. You could call Occidental's public relations department, tell them you're interested in learning about their company as a potential investor, and have them send you their annual reports, quarterly reports, and any other relevant material. You may even find they have company tours, which are often interesting and can be helpful. Then you can study the company's relation to the rest of the industry. You could then compare Occidental's possibilities—as gleaned from what it says about itself, as well as from information you can gather from more objective sources, such as the financial pages of your newspaper—with those in other investment areas, such as electronics or pharmaceuticals.

A good example of the advantage of proximity is the group of Twin Cities people who originally sensed the possibilities of the Minnesota Mining and Manufacturing (3M) Company and bought stock when it was just starting to roll. Many of these investors were inspired by young 3M executives who told them how the company was engaging in highly creative research, bringing out attractive new products, advertising and marketing them in a venturesome way. Thus they got onto a tremendous growth possibility early, and in a decade or so found themselves getting rich from the steady rise of 3M stock.

The togetherness way of investing in the stock market, one that appeals to many people because of both the social aspect and the security afforded by numbers and group decisions, is to join an investment club.

Depending on your temperament—that is, how group-minded you are—the investment club can be a good thing. You needn't sink a lot of money into your joint ventures, and there is the fun of combined planning, the shared joy of successful investment.

I'm not a joiner myself; I find the greatest stimulation in what I can achieve on my own. Also, I can see disadvantages in joining an investment club. There are seldom professionals directly involved, and I doubt whether the membership would be as highly venturesome as I consider myself to be.

But for many women, especially those with limited funds available for investment, the clubs constitute an excellent introduction to the financial world.

There are all sorts of groupings, some clubs having "men only" or "women only" rules, some composed of married couples, or senior citizens, or young people, or members of the same religious, social, or professional organizations. The total number of investment clubs is estimated at around 20,000. Of that number about 13,000 are affiliated with the National Association of Investment Clubs, which was founded in 1951 as a nonprofit organization.

Each club, whether affiliated with the NAIC or not, decides what investments it wants to make and then calls in a broker to handle the details. Membership in the NAIC costs each club $30 a year plus $1 for each member, in return for which the club receives the guidelines for operating as an investment group, a $25,000 fidelity bond for the club, and a subscription for each member to the association's monthly magazine, *Better Investing*. (A fidelity bond is the document issued by a bonding or insurance company guaranteeing to make good the fraud of a member of an organization covered by the bond.)

The principal idea behind the NAIC formula for group success is that all dividends and capital gains from the sale of any stock held in the club's portfolio will be reinvested rather than paid out immediately to the individual members. The claim is made that a member of a typical club who invests $20 a month will have a $20,000 share of the club's assets in about a score of years. In any case, the members are advised to invest a certain sum each month, and withdraw any accumulated holdings only in an emergency. A member can invest a $10 unit per month—the usual minimum—or several units of $10 each, but generally a maximum is set to prevent wealthier members from dominating a group.

Some clubs operate through an investment committee with a chairman and several members, the makeup of which is rotated every three or four months. This committee evaluates several growth stocks each month. Some are referred to it for study by the club's broker or by members who have picked up useful information. The committee reports on its evaluations at the monthly meetings, and the membership votes on whether to follow the committee's recommendations. Many clubs also have a portfolio management committee, which reports monthly on the current value of each stock held by the club.

Since most people join investment clubs that are affiliated with the NAIC, it might be helpful to you in deciding whether to join such a group to know what the association recommends for its affiliates. The NAIC suggests that investments be made on a regular basis, regardless of the fluctuations of the market; if it's down, and the club's portfolio has accordingly depreciated, you still keep investing $10, $20, or whatever each month. All earnings should be reinvested to compound the portfolio's value. Investments should be diversified among various companies and industries. The main emphasis is on buying growth stocks, if possible when they start their climb, a growth stock being defined as one that increases in value faster than the economy as a whole.

Naturally the success of the clubs varies, depending on the combined acumen of their memberships. They can provide the social excitement of the shared risk. Put more bluntly, you don't feel quite so bad about losing money if a number of other people have suffered equally. The other side of the coin is that you can all rejoice together when things are going well. The socializing, I suspect, is half the fun of the investment clubs. Certainly they provide an opportunity to invest in the market at no great risk for women without a lot to venture, or who are cautious and conservative by nature.

12 /

Aggressive Money

Let's say you've filled in most of the lower blocks in your Financial Planning Pyramid by now. You've stashed four to six months' income in a savings account. You have adequate personal insurance and own your own house; you've picked up a few Treasury bills or certificates of deposit. If being part of an investment club or a mutual fund nest egg holds no charms for you and you're determined to win your economic independence through your own efforts, you'll already have given serious thought to entering the field of aggressive money. That's where the creative action is. You should remember, however, that stocks and the stock market are in fact aggressive investments, and should not be entered until all the bottom blocks of your pyramid are filled in. All too often people want to start in by taking a flier in the market—and very rarely do they make it.

Don't neglect your reading: the *Wall Street Journal, Barron's, Forbes,* or *Business Week,* the financial pages of the *New York Times* and other leading papers. Most financial publications write about exciting things that aggressive business people have *made* happen. You will also find that the *Wall Street Journal* now has a very positive attitude toward women, frequently featuring articles about them on its front page. These publications are not as "heavy" as you might think. By this time, too, you'll have mastered the supposedly esoteric terminology of the market and the various strategies for increasing your net worth through risk investment rather than saving. You'll also have picked up some of the intense competitive joy of winning your place in the market, of managing your own money and therefore your future independence.

All the jargon will have become as familiar to you as the names of the standard brands in the supermarket. You'll know that when people refer to the day's DJIA or "Dow," it's the Dow Jones Industrial Average—a function of the prices of a certain 30 companies' stocks that day—which is the oldest indicator of how the market is moving as a whole, the key figure mentioned in newspaper headlines and nightly television news programs. This is a hotly contested subject. Is the performance of 30 stocks out of thousands a true indicator? Well, it *is* an indicator, and one to be watched just because it's there. You should recognize that the Dow Jones Industrial Average is not the most representative average of the market as a whole. Newer and more all-inclusive averages have been developed more recently, such as the New York Stock Exchange Composite Index and the *Standard and Poor's* 500, both much broader than the 30 industrials included in the DJIA. However, long history and popularity still make the DJIA the most widely quoted and used index among members of the investing public.

You'll know the difference between "bid" and "asked," bid being the highest price anyone is offering to pay for a certain stock, asked being the lowest price at which anyone is willing to sell it at a given time. You'll know that "blue chips" are the common stock of the largest corporations with good earnings and regular dividends. That "averaging up" means buying more of a certain issue as its price goes up, and "averaging down" means buying more of that issue as its price falls. That "book value" signifies the net worth that backs up a company's common stock (stockholders' equity divided by number of common shares outstanding). That "dollar stocks" are low-price, highly speculative issues selling for less than $10 a share. That "buying on margin" means buying listed stocks by making a down payment—the amount regulated by the Federal Reserve Bank—on the full price of a stock, the balance being borrowed from your brokerage at a certain interest rate. That "preferred stock" is one on which a company must pay dividends before doing so on common stock. That "daily quotations," as published in your newspaper's financial section, refers to the previous day's highest, lowest, and closing prices paid for stocks on the various exchanges.

By then, too, you'll understand just how the trading process works, from the moment you phone your broker with a decision to buy a certain stock to the moment the transaction is completed. The stock exchange works the same way as an auction market.

Let's say that you've decided, after consultation with your broker, to buy 100 shares of National Electric (a mythical corporation). He'll probably push a button on the console on his desk to receive a reading on a screen showing that the last sale of National Electric was at 44½, meaning $44.50 a share. You agree to buy it at that price, or he may suggest that you place an order for the stock at a slightly lower quotation, 44⅜, to "see if we get any bids," this being a "good till canceled order." Or he may place a "day order," which means the price you bid is good for that day only, and if that price isn't reached in the day's trading it would have to be renewed the following day.

Your order for 100 shares of National Electric then goes to the brokerage's order room, from which it is telegraphed to the firm's head office in New York, if it has one, or to the broker's representative on the floor of the New York Stock Exchange.

A clerk receives the order and turns it over to the floor broker, who heads immediately for the appropriate trading post. The nearly 2,000 stocks listed on the New York Stock Exchange are divided up among its 22 trading posts. Let's say National Electric is traded at Post 7. At this station the floor broker with your order joins a group of men—often shouting or gesturing violently—gathered around a "specialist," a broker wearing a special jacket who specializes in trading National Electric and a small number of other stocks. It is the specialist's function to make an "orderly market" in the stocks for which he has responsibility. This means that he keeps an "order book" in which he enters both the bids to buy the stock and any offers to sell the stock, and matches buyers with sellers at prices on which they can both agree.

In those cases where the bid and the ask prices are so far apart that a potential buyer and seller cannot get together and agree on a price, it is the specialist's function to purchase or sell the stock for his own personal account at a price somewhere between the most recent bid and ask prices, and thus personally to create what is referred to as an "orderly market." The function of the specialist is presently a very controversial subject, and the next several years may well see fundamental changes in this area.

The specialist quotes to your broker's representative the going price for the stock. If you've instructed your broker to place a market order—that is, at the current quotation—his representative will tell the specialist he wants 100 shares at that price. If, on the other hand, you and your broker have decided to place a "good till canceled order" or a "day order," the specialist will note the price you're willing to pay in his notebook and fill the order if and when the price reaches the level you've designated.

Word that your order has been filled is telegraphed to your broker. Often within an hour you will be informed that you are the owner of 100 shares of National Electric. You then have five working days in which to give your broker a check to complete the transaction.

These, in brief, are the mechanics of buying a stock listed on one of the major exchanges. It's a little different in dealing with over-the-counter (OTC) stocks, which represent companies generally not yet mature or successful enough to be traded on one of the major exchanges. Major exceptions include American Express and many large banks, which are traded OTC.

Say you're interested in an OTC stock selling for around $12 a share. You call your broker and ask for the current quotations. It's a good thing to remember that the spread between "bid" and "ask" price in the OTC market is generally a lot wider than on the American or New York Stock Exchange issues. Your broker may tell you the bid is 11⅞ for the stock you're interested in, and the asking price is 12¼. That's a big spread. That means the people owning the stock are willing to sell it for $12.25 while people buying the stock are willing to pay $11.87 a share. If your broker places an order with a ceiling of 12⅛, or $12.13, the chances are excellent that you will be able to buy it at the compromise price. The less frequently traded an OTC stock is, the wider the spread between the bid and ask prices.

One drawback to dealing over the counter is the larger spread. It is also customary for some over-the-counter dealers to buy and sell certain stocks for their own account. Often the profit or spread they make on such transactions, or the commission they charge on OTC transactions, is greater than a commission in a New York Stock Exchange transaction would be. The brokers' commission structure is presently undergoing fundamental changes. Ask your broker in advance what the brokerage fee is. It varies.

There are so many struggling for their share of the available capital to expand and eventually to reach Big Board status that the OTC market, in aggregate, is many times larger than that of the major exchanges. Many of the fastest growth businesses have their stocks sold over the counter. Often, too, the OTC stocks represent long-entrenched and conservatively managed companies operating only in a certain locality or region. Such localized concerns would include banks, water and power companies, independent electric light companies, machine shops, bus lines, and the whole range of commerce and industry that is too remote or obscure to attract the attention of Wall Street. You might say they comprise the minor leagues of finance, but many dramatic successes have emerged and will emerge from their ranks.

•

Many women inexperienced in the ways of the financial world have asked me, "But isn't buying stocks just like playing the crap tables at Las Vegas?" They've heard of the speculative side of stock investment, of paper fortunes made and lost, of people "ruined" in the 1929 crash because they'd bought stocks on margin and had to sell everything they owned to pay what they owed a broker for buying stocks with a 10 percent down payment and the balance borrowed from the broker.

The days of reckless speculation in margin accounts are over; at this writing the Securities and Exchange Commission has set the margin level at 50 percent to discourage such headlong dicing. (Even so, margin purchases still remain a problem; when margin calls went out during a recent market break, a lot of people got hurt. Be wary of the broker who urges a lot of margin action.)

But you could hardly call buying quality stocks or collecting dividends "gambling." Whatever the rise or fall of a stock's market price, you still own those shares and receive the dividends on them. Naturally, you can lose money if you sell the stock at a lower price than you paid for it. If you hang on to it until its value has recovered (if it does), you've suffered only a paper loss during the period the stock is in decline.

As G. M. Loeb has written in perhaps the best book dealing with the stock market, *The Battle for Investment Survival* (first published in 1935 but reprinted many times since and still fresh and valid):

Accepting losses is the most important single investment device to insure safety of capital. It is also the action that most people know the least about and that they are least liable to execute. . . . The most important single thing I have learned is that accepting losses promptly is the first key to success.

In other words, when the stock drops below your buy price, don't let it ride in hopes of its going back up. Cut your losses fast—sell!

Mr. Loeb, whose immense authority was derived from half a century in the money game and a senior partnership in E. F. Hutton and Company, exemplifies what I mean about "aggressive money," the determination to make money work for you and secure a comfortable future. To be aggressive in the money sense, you have to be resilient enough to accept losses and failures, certain in the knowledge that this is the only way you're going to liberate yourself financially.

To quote Mr. Loeb again:

Deliberate, planned speculation is, in my opinion, the best and safest method to improve one's chances of preserving the purchasing power of capital or maintaining its constant convertibility into cash without loss. . . . There is only one intelligent approach to the employment or protection of capital, and that is to *use it for profit* . . . [italics mine].

And he sums up exactly what I define as the method of running aggressive money:

Aim at a real profit. Reject everything that does not promise to advance generously in price. *Keep cash* if enough issues cannot be found or if the investment per issue becomes unwieldy. Shares purchased for a big profit may be sold long before the original goal is achieved. . . . *Keep uninvested* unless and until a particularly opportune time presents itself. . . . Nevertheless, mistakes will be made. And when they are, there is no cheaper insurance than accepting a loss quickly. . . .

The only way to succeed in venturesome management of your life a lot more fun, by creatively using the generating spare to the project. You can't think of your capital as an egg waiting to be hatched by others. Money is now your avocation, if not your vocation; as such, it has to be given the same kind of personal attention a mother would devote to her children. The more mental energy you put into your money management—the more analyzing and studying and investigating you do, the more time you spend reading the *Wall Street Journal* and financial pages, observing the fluctuations of the market in the flyspeck print of the day's Wall Street quotations—the quicker you will free yourself from the gritty concerns of paying bills, sweating over budgets, and worrying about inflation. You can avoid such daily afflictions, and make your life a lot more fun, by creatively using the generating power of money intelligently invested. You have to *care*, and you should care if your own future means anything to you.

Which brings me to the sad story of a friend of mine. Fifteen years ago she sold a house and realized a tidy profit on the transaction. She decided to invest the money in stock, felt attracted to Technicolor, Inc., and learned that it was selling for only $7 a share.

Right after she bought 3,000 shares at 7 there was a boom in Technicolor film production and the stock began to soar. When it reached 26 she decided to bail out, her holdings having almost quadrupled in value. (Actually she'd have made a bigger killing if she'd held on to the stock a bit longer; it went up into the 40s. But it's always better to sell too soon than too late.)

What happened was that Maggie suffered from an attack of overoptimism. It was the mid-sixties, the economy was surging forward, and the economists were all talking confidently about how they'd arranged permanent prosperity for the country. Instead of working at building up her investment portfolio, Maggie carelessly distributed her capital in a number of undistinguished stocks and took off for Europe. With everything booming, one stock seemed as good as another; it was out-of-sight, out-of-mind time. She enjoyed herself so much in Europe that after she'd returned home she decided to travel in the other direction and make it around the world.

Maggie was in the Punjab when she got the bad news from

Wall Street. The bottom had dropped out of her stocks, along with a lot of others. It was back to reality for Maggie—and back to work, too. You take a cavalier attitude toward money at your peril.

Eternal vigilance isn't only the price of liberty; it's the gate toll to solvency and self-realization. You *must* keep studying, analyzing, changing your position if necessary; never, never take the market for granted. Enjoy the financial pages as you do a crossword puzzle or a bridge game.

Actually there's a sequel to Maggie's tragic tale, and it's every bit as instructive. Because she had risen to fortune on Technicolor, Inc., she developed an emotional attachment to that stock—not as odd a phenomenon as you might think. For no good reason she bought back into it after she'd raised some capital again—and let herself be hoodwinked into reinvesting every time she would sell something. You must learn to say no: If you've decided to sell out, *do it* and pick up the money. Don't be conned into reinvesting in another stock—by yourself, or by your broker.

The generative power of money is something that women in the past have sometimes found difficult to grasp. All too often money means a thin sheaf of currency in the purse, or figures noted in a bank's checkbook. Something inert, lifeless, static. Something, in effect, to be ignored until you need it to pay for the groceries or for a fling in Barbados (or, worse yet, something that isn't there when you need it).

To illustrate this "generative power" I'm talking about, a celebrated New York banker years ago made an interesting projection, based on the fact that capital compounded at 5 percent doubles itself in a little more than 14 years. If the wealthy Medici family in Italy six centuries ago had set aside, at 5 percent compound interest, an investment fund equal to $100,000, by 1933 that fund would have increased in value to $517,000,000,000,000,000 ($517 quadrillion), or 46 million times the existing monetary gold supply in the whole world.

I'm not suggesting that you set your mind on founding a

Medici-type dynasty, but you should be aware of the fact that only through investment can you protect yourself against the greater threat to preserving your capital—the constant variation in the purchasing power of money caused by such factors as inflation, rising rates of taxation, government regulation, war, changes in the political and economic climate, and social unrest.

Creative investment is your way, in essence, of protecting what you've worked for, saved, worried over. And you are protecting your family as well. It isn't an expression of greed, or wanting to snatch what others have, or merely "money-grubbing," as the lazy and envious like to call it.

You have to observe a stock's behavior much as you watch over and correct a child's conduct to make sure he/she doesn't slip into delinquency.

Once you've bought stock in a company, you should keep careful tabs on its dividends policy. Dividends are not always consistent, and dividend policy varies, of course, from company to company. When you bought the stock, you were probably told it had paid, say, $10 a year for the past *x* years. But you can't count on getting $10 annually for every share you own. Some companies stick like bonding glue to their proclaimed dividend rate and regard it as something sacrosanct, not to be affected by a slump in business or other disasters. Others will decide, in board meetings in which you have no part, that the dividend must be lowered for a certain year, or skipped altogether if the company's financial situation is suffering.

You'll have to keep an eye on your investment to determine just how faithful the company is about paying out dividends.

And if dividend payments become erratic over the course of a few years, you should take a hard look at whether or not to keep your money tied up in that company's future.

Many companies, as you may find out too late if you're counting on strictly cash dividends, pay off in shares of stock, or a mixture of cash and stock. This is often true of growing companies that want to hold on to their cash reserves and use them for expansion or increased operating expenses.

Though people often feel they are getting a break through stock dividends, they really may not be. Suppose you hold 100 shares in our mythical National Electric for which you paid $45 a share, or a total of $4,500. If National Electric declares a 5 percent stock dividend, and you thus receive five more shares of the company, that doesn't mean you've received the equivalent of $225. You now have 105 shares instead of 100, but your total investment is still $4,500 and your holdings still represent the same percentage of ownership in the company as your 100 shares did. You'll stand to gain, of course, if the price of the company's stock does not drop because of the stock dividend.

A stock split is different from a stock dividend, though the two are closely related. Again the benefit is more psychological than mathematical; but the shareholders in a growth company like the splits because they are usually performed by companies whose earnings are on the rise, and they are taken as a sign that the company is really growing.

Suppose National Electric announces a two-for-one stock split. Your 100 shares are increased to 200. But they still represent the same percentage of ownership in the company. The market value per share of your stock usually is halved when a stock split is announced. Sometimes it is a little more than half, and you have a margin of profit, on paper, further increased if investors push up the price.

The close relationship between stock dividends and stock splits is indicated by the fact that the New York Stock Exchange considers anything less than a 20 percent stock distribution a dividend; anything over that figure a stock split. Many brokers and analysts contend that there is a built-in psychological factor here—that stock-splitting draws in a lot of investors who feel they're picking up a bargain, "getting in on the ground floor."

What should be included in your portfolio? That can be

answered only in generalizations, since all of us differ in age, education, career possibilities, and earned or inherited income; no woman's situation is exactly like another's.

If your circumstances dictate a conservative approach, you'll naturally want a mixture of stocks and bonds that guarantee a steady income. Most career women, fairly young and with good prospects, will or should want to be more adventurous. Even those with family responsibilities, many experts now believe, should take a more aggressive attitude toward managing their capital.

As Charles J. Rolo, the financial writer and portfolio manager, says (in line with G. M. Loeb's dictum), "My conviction is that the best way to preserve capital is to manage it aggressively. When a client has insisted on high yields as a primary consideration, the account has turned in a disappointing performance. On the other hand, a number of clients have agreed to let me give them a monthly basic income they might require from the account and let me manage it primarily to achieve capital gains. . . . It is my belief that under reasonably favorable overall conditions, a portfolio invested in this way can show an average appreciation of 10 to 18 percent annually. Obviously in bear-market years, the portfolio would be likely to show a decline, but this could be made up in strong bull markets."

You should manage your own portfolio, of course, unless your holdings are so large that they require a professional, in which case you probably wouldn't be reading this book. Use your own judgment, based on study and research. Don't invest all your money in a few stocks but aim for a mix. Keep careful records of how each stock performs so that you'll be up to the minute on their prospects in the market.

Experts generally agree that there are several guidelines to be followed by practically all investors with fair-sized portfolios (this would not apply if you're just venturing into the money world and have only a few thousand dollars to invest):

1. You should have about 20 to 25 percent of your portfolio invested in "good" stocks with steady track records.

2. A cash reserve is advisable for purchase of bargains in the market that might crop up suddenly.

3. You *don't* always have to be in the game. If making money in a particular market is unlikely, you should just get out and lie low until another opportunity arises. (You always need to be evaluating your investments in terms of the risk-reward ratio. For instance, when interest rates are high, people tend to stay out of the market. The reason for this is that you can get safer—and perhaps equivalent—returns from Treasury bills, certificates of deposit, and so on.)

4. Make sure your holdings are growing in value. You should expect a 10 percent increase in value (appreciation plus dividends) on the sounder stocks annually, a 15 percent rate on the more speculative ones—at least when the market is trending upward.

That way your little golf go-cart will keep up with or gain on that 11 m.p.h. conveyor belt. And that is the object of the game. A woman may learn that nothing is much more stimulating—to her mind, her career, or her future—than aggressive money handling. If she's skillful she can make it all the way.

The losses you incur on your stock transactions can be offset against your gains. Specifically, short-term losses (on stock held not more than six months) can be offset against short-term gains, and long-term losses against long-term gains. Net short-term gains (after deducting short-term losses) are taxable at essentially the same rate as ordinary income, whereas net long-term net gains are generally taxable at approximately half that rate. Any excess loss over gains in a year is deductible from ordinary income only to the extent of $1,000 per year.

MUTUAL FUNDS

Because it is difficult to predict the behavior of any particular stock, or even to forecast the trends in the stock market, mutual funds were established to take some of the risk out of stock ownership. A mutual fund is a professionally managed portfolio of many different stocks and/or bonds, the theory being that if the risk is spread over a wide range of companies and industries, a disaster to one company or a downturn in one industry won't greatly harm the owner of mutual fund shares. One reason for the mutual funds' great rise during the sixties was that many of the larger brokerages, swamped by bookkeeping and rising overheads, began ignoring the smaller investor whose commissions weren't worth the expense and paper work involved. Early in the seventies, however, the sharp fall in the market resulted in some disillusionment with mutual funds, their shareholders having learned that professional management couldn't shield them from the vagaries of the market.

During the go-go years brokers encouraged the growth of mutual funds because they received higher commissions on mutual fund transactions than on handling odd lots (less than multiples of 100 shares) of stock for small investors. Many people interested in stock investment found themselves talked into joining a mutual fund by their brokers—often, in those days, to the investor's profit.

One major problem with many mutual funds is the "loading" charge, generally 8 percent of the investment—more than the investor would pay for buying his own stocks. There are, however, "no-load" funds that make no such charges. The funds with a load policy are aggressively promoted by a direct sales force. The no-load funds make out on modest advertising budgets or depend heavily on word of mouth. Obviously the trick is to find a no-load fund with a good performance record and avoid being penalized 8 percent. The current trend among the mutuals is toward conversion to a no-load policy.

With most mutual funds you are, in effect, paying a group of professionals to handle your money for you (typically for a fee of 1 percent or so per year), to stand between you and your investments. Your financial fortunes are dependent on their sagacity, which should be greater than the average layman's.

Most of the mutuals are "open-end" funds, which means they are continually selling new shares in their operations and enlarging their portfolios of securities. If the shareholder wants to liquidate some or all of his holdings, the fund buys back his interest in the combined portfolio at the market value of the day of the repurchase.

One problem with the large successful funds—and some are huge—is the difficulty they have in buying and selling very large blocks of stock without affecting the market price unfavorably. Small funds do not suffer from this phenomenon.

During the past three decades the performance of the mutual funds was excellent in a rising stock market, as was that of many individual investors. Compared to the Dow-Jones Index during the early seventies, however, the mutuals as a whole haven't performed very well. Their track records vary widely. Thus you should study the record of any specific fund that attracts you in publications such as the *Wiesenberg Report*, realizing that a good performance in the past doesn't guarantee one for the future.

The fund takes the money of its shareholders and invests in areas it regards as promising, mostly common stocks, with bonds mixed in for stability in certain funds. It keeps enough cash on hand to pay off shareholders withdrawing from the fund. The mutuals as a whole were badly punished by redemptions in the early seventies.

The mutual funds have differing investment policies and personalities. Some are "go-go" types with an appetite for speculative or high-risk areas. Others place primary emphasis on safeguarding the portfolio from losses, and will probably have a higher content of bonds and debentures than the funds that aim to achieve higher capital gains.

If you're oriented toward mutual fund investment, you should decide whether you're more interested in a growth fund, largely devoted to common stocks with a dramatic potential, or an income fund, which invests in companies that pay high and regular dividends.

As an experiment, you might buy a certain number of shares in a mutual fund while allotting the rest of your investment capital to buying stocks on your own. Then compare, at the end of a year or two, how well the fund has done against your own profit or loss. Perhaps you'll find yourself in agreement with Donald Regan, president of the Merrill Lynch brokerage firm, who believes that the individual investor can do better on his own than by entrusting his financial fate to a mutual fund.

Still, it must be admitted that the mutuals have their virtues. For anyone who does not have the talent or cannot give the requisite time to managing her own investment portfolio, the mutuals have generally performed well over the distance. While few have made a killing in the mutuals, no one I know has been wiped out, either.

13 /

The Gilt-edged World

The term "gilt-edged" is often applied to debentures and bonds, not only because of the elaborate imitation gold-leaf scrollwork that adorned them in former days, but because this type of securities is considered very safe. Bonds may be boring compared to stocks, but many investors would rather be safe than sorry. They are government or corporate IOUS, a promise on the part of the issuer to repay the amount invested by a certain date, in return for which you receive regular interest payments. Bonds are not 100 percent safe, however, since the company, municipality, or utility can, in fact, go bankrupt. (A grim current example is New York City.)

What's the difference between a stock and a bond? A stockholder is in effect a part owner of a company in which he has invested. A bondholder is a creditor of the company whose investment is usually secured by a specific asset pledged for this purpose, such as real estate, rolling stock, and so on. This secures the creditor in case the company has difficulty in paying off the bond when it matures. If a company goes broke, the bondholders are paid off before the stockholders. Since the latter take the larger risk, they may expect a larger return on their investment.

A *debenture* is an unsecured bond, a corporation's long-term promissory note. It is not secured by a specific asset but is an unsecured general obligation of the company. Debentures are sometimes considered a special class of bond. Like a bondholder, the owner of a debenture is the creditor of the issuing company and cannot vote on company business, as a stockholder does. A *convertible debenture* is somewhat differ-ent—I'll discuss it later on in this chapter.

Bonds and debentures are not particularly attractive to me, as compared with stocks, because they are not an aggres-sive form of investment. I tend to agree with G. M. Loeb that

...bonds of any grade are only occasionally useful in the informed investor's portfolio. . . . It is difficult to get advice on them. Bond houses usually concentrate on the issues on their shelves. Brokers find the commission too low and are too busy to give them careful study for the negligible remuneration.

Yet bonds are powerfully attractive to some investors, and there are several hundred specialists in bond sales throughout the country who find buyers for billions of dollars' worth of such securities every year.

The prices of issued and outstanding bonds fluctuate for various reasons, but the overall trend of the bond market is primarily determined by long-term interest rate levels. If the interest rates offered by new bond issues are rising, prices of older bond issues drop to equalize the return offered. If long-term interest rates are heading down, however, out-standing bonds become much more attractive to the investor since their prices are rising.

The problem with bonds (as with many other investments) is that their after-tax yield may not keep pace with inflation. For example: Let's say an 8 percent bond is selling at face value. The taxpayer is in the 30 percent bracket. Her after-tax net yield is 5.6 percent (70 percent of 8 percent). If inflation is running at, say, 9 percent per year, she is losing purchasing power at the rate of 3.4 percent per year. Bad news, over the long pull.

Nevertheless, bonds are one of the most popular instru-ments of debt financing for cities, utilities, and major com-panies. And bonds do differ widely—which is why they are rated by a coding system in *Moody's* and *Standard and Poor.* These two rating services can be found at your stockbroker's or your public library. The rating system runs from AAA (best) down to A; then BBB ranging down to B. Mr. Loeb's advice is to buy only AAA bonds; otherwise (and I agree) you are running a risk equivalent to investing in a stock without any upside potential, because bonds are set at a fixed return, and stocks are of course open-ended.

This is roughly how the bond market works:

Our favorite example, National Electric Corporation, is selling bonds at $1,000 each with a fixed interest rate of 8 percent, or $80 per year. If interest rates rise and National Electric's rivals in the bond market begin offering new bonds at 10 percent interest, or $100 a year, those older National Electric bonds could drop in market value to about $800. At that lower price National Electric's fixed interest payment, still $80 a year, would amount to a current yield of 10 percent for every person who bought a bond at $800.

If a bondholder keeps the bond until it matures—that is, until the date it must be paid off—he will get $1,000 back from the issuer in addition to the interest he receives every year until it matures. Thus the "yield to maturity"—taking into account the final repayment of the bond itself—will be different from the "current yield," represented by the interest alone. A woman who bought a National Electric $1,000 bond for $800 on a temporarily declining market, therefore, would have a $200 capital gain *plus* the annual interest at maturity.

There are three general types of bonds on the market:

1. *Corporate* bonds, issued by business firms.

2. *Municipal* bonds, issued by local and state governments to finance various projects.

3. *U.S. government* bonds, which are direct obligations of the Treasury, and other federal issues offered separately by government agencies.

All types of bonds, in fact, are issued to raise money for certain purposes. The American Telephone and Telegraph Company will float a bond issue to expand the telephone system. Your own city government will issue bonds to build, say, a new sewage disposal plant. Both private companies and government agencies usually would have been able to borrow money from the banks, but for various reasons they often find it less costly to enter the bond market for the capital they require.

The bond market may seem to be one of the more staid sectors of the money world, but it does a brisk business. Every day, up to a dozen new corporate and municipal bond issues are offered the investing public. And that's in addition to a constant turnover in older issues.

To give you some size of the market, the statistics for 1973 show that corporations sold $13.5 billion worth of bonds that year, while state and local governments issued a total of $22.7 billion and the U.S. Treasury about $35 billion.

A good proportion of the issues are bought by various institutions, but there's plenty of action left for the private investor. Bond-buying is heavily favored by insurance companies, banks, credit unions, mutual funds, pension funds, and labor unions, all with large amounts of money traditionally invested in the more conservative securities.

It's the safety factor that attracts all that money which has to be diverted, often by law, to the sure-thing kind of investment. That sure-thing factor, too, would influence you if, say, your husband is incapacitated or there is serious illness in your family, or you're a widowed or divorced mother with children. If not, you'll be looking for a higher rate of return on your money.

The institutional investors, burdened with responsibilities as they are, operate cautiously even in the safety zone represented by the bond market. Some institutions are required by law to invest only in government or municipal bonds, while insurance companies generally favor corporate bonds because they offer a higher return. Since securities issued by the U.S. government are regarded as the safest of all bonds, they offer a lower interest rate. On bonds issued by state or local governments, the interest is usually lower than that on federal government or corporate bonds, but they have an important fringe benefit: There is no federal tax payable on the interest from municipal bonds, and usually there is no state income tax payable on bonds issued in the state of the bondholder's residence. If a taxpayer is in the 50 percent bracket and purchases a municipal bond with a 5 percent interest coupon, this is equivalent to interest on a regular bond paying 10 percent, since half of that interest would be payable in federal income taxes. The actual return (after taxes) is therefore higher than it is for federal issues.

What are the comparative rates of interest offered by various types of bonds? They fluctuate to some degree, depending on the state of the bond market. The readings for a recent day will give you some idea of their returns. High-quality corporate bonds were offering 8.40 percent annual interest—less than the rate of inflation—while federal government issues were paying 6.91 percent and state or municipal bonds 6.01 (I'm not figuring in tax breaks).

There is a considerable spread in the interest rates offered by corporate bond issues and, of equal importance to the prospective investor, in the financial soundness of the companies issuing them.

A good rule of thumb: The larger and stronger company is a safer investment than a struggling concern—but it will also yield a lower return in interest.

You can find out just how safe a corporate bond is by consulting one of several independent credit rating services that assess new bond issues with the same cold practiced eye as a loan officer surveying an applicant for a personal loan. A triple-A rating is given those companies with the soundest financial structure. The least favorable assessment is a C rating. In between are a half-dozen other classifications. Your broker can give you complete information on the bond rating by *Standard and Poor* or *Moody's*.

There are several interesting ventures in the federal sector of the bond market; you may have heard about them if you travel with people who favor that kind of investment. One is called "Fannie Maes," and even their Wall Street nickname makes them attractive to fairly conservative investors.

Fannie Maes are bonds issued by a government agency, the Federal National Mortgage Association (FNMA), which encourages home building by buying and selling mortgages to and from banks, savings and loan companies, and real estate combines. When a bank, for instance, wants to liquidate some of its mortgages, it can sell them to the FNMA, which (at least until recently) makes home financing more attractive to lending institutions. To finance such operations, the FNMA sells notes or debentures to the public in amounts ranging from $1,000 to $10,000. They have the advantage of occasionally comfortable yields and the plus factor of being easily liquidated in the market.

Compared to the tumult of a stock exchange floor, the bond market is a fairly sedate and quiet-running institution. A typical bond firm in downtown Los Angeles has four salesmen who spend most of their time on the telephone, calling their accounts and advising them of new issues just placed on the market.

In one corner of the salesman's office is a loudspeaker hooked up to a direct phone line to the firm's New York office. A woman's voice comes over the line announcing that their firm is one of a group that has made the successful low bid for a new bond issue from a Wisconsin utility company. That means the firm is one of several that will market the bonds to individual investors.

One of the salesmen immediately gets on the phone to one of his customers, a Los Angeles bank that buys large amounts of bonds for its trust department. He tells the banker that the Wisconsin utility bond is available at 8.65 percent interest. Let's say he gets a turndown—the bank is interested only in larger issues.

Another salesman is on the phone to the trading desk of the firm's New York headquarters trying to obtain, for a client's benefit, the latest quotations on several bonds in the secondary market—that is, older bonds released from their original price restrictions and thus subject to fluctuations in the market.

It's a low-keyed business, dealing in bonds; no electronic tape recording of the latest price flutters on the Big Board back in New York; not much excitement, because the traders do business mainly with banks, pension funds, and other conservative institutions. Hours pass before there's a stir of triumph in the room—one of the salesmen has sold 50 bonds of a new issue to the manager of a northern California retirement fund.

In this same area, but offering a little more excitement for the investor, there's the *convertible debenture*. An ordinary debenture, like a bond, is a company's IOU. A convertible debenture differs in that it can be transformed into common stock issued by the company at a fixed price.

Say you've bought a debenture issued by National Electric for $1,000. It can be converted into 40 shares of common stock, which makes the conversion price $25 a share.

If National Electric's common stock rises to $36 a share, and you have the conversion privilege, converting the debenture gives you an $11 profit on each of your 40 shares. This happy turn of events, of course, would be reflected in the market value of National Electric's convertible debentures. And that's the beauty of buying such issues. If the company's common stock rises, you can profit through conversion. If it doesn't, you still have the interest coming in on the unconverted debenture—though if the common stock drops sharply, the market value of the issue will also be depreciated.

·

Bond prices simply don't move up and down as dramatically as stock market offerings. For those who like to operate aggressively in the money world, this is a quiet backwater. It's not to be ignored, however, if you want a safe shelter for your funds during a certain period. As Gerald Loeb points out, there is little point to buying bonds offering a low yield when "the cost of living has risen to such an extent that the total of interest and repaid principal in currency will buy only as much as or less than the principal itself at the time of the bond purchase." And *he* was writing back in the mid-thirties, when a movie cost a quarter and you could get a good meal for less than a dollar!

14 /

Other Investment Ventures and Adventures

For only the most sophisticated and daring among investors there is a method of speculation called *options,* which consists of three different concepts mysteriously called *calls, puts,* and *straddles.* These are all various types of options that have totally different functions. The options market has been around for over a century, but has recently taken on new popularity and interest. However, no beginner should venture into this area, nor should anyone with a limited amount of capital, or who can't afford to take high risks. We're on the summit of that financial planning pyramid now, where the winds are violent and the footing precarious. Options are not for the conservative or faint of heart.

Generally these offshoots of the stock market deal with options to buy or sell common stocks at predetermined prices. You're betting, in effect, on the future rise or fall of the price of the underlying stock.

A *call* is an option to buy 100 shares of a stock, usually listed on the New York Stock Exchange, at a prearranged price within a certain period (usually several months). The buyer of a call is therefore betting the stock will rise. A *put* is just the opposite: an option to sell that stock at a certain price. The buyer expects the stock to drop so he can buy it in the open market at a price less than his put price. The third option is termed a *straddle,* which is a simultaneous put and call.

Therefore, the straddle buyer is betting that the stock will go either up or down *sharply;* in either case he makes money.

This is the way it works: You pay a small amount of money called a *premium* for a much larger amount of stock than is represented by the premium. You don't actually own the stock, merely an option on buying or selling it. You choose whether and when to exercise the option. If the stock doesn't move in the direction you thought it would, you simply drop the option and lose the premium, a matter perhaps of a few hundred dollars. One advantage of puts and calls is that you know exactly how much you stand to lose—the premium only; another is that they can be used to hedge your stock holdings in a falling market.

For sophisticated investors, such option trading is becoming undeniably more attractive, to the extent that recently there was established the Chicago Board Options Exchange, a market that deals only in options to buy or sell stock. Even more recently a similar service has also been provided by the American Stock Exchange.

Since I haven't dealt in stock options myself, I can only quote the CBOE's claim that it "streamlines the processing of options trades" and accomplishes a "breakthrough" by creating "a secondary market in which holders and writers of CBOE options should be able to transfer their interest in an option contract at a price that reflects the amount of time it still has to run." Until now, the Chicago exchange explains, "options have been dealt in without the availability of such a secondary market," but now a "call option takes on the attributes of a full-fledged security whose market characteristics should resemble those of a short-term warrant."

A warrant, which is considered the most conservative type of option, can be described as a long-term "call." It is an option to buy a stock at a specific price over a long period of time (vs. a call which is short term), in some cases an indefinite period of time. Warrants often grow out of initial stock or bond offerings.

The CBOE is candid in stating that its offerings aren't for everyone.

If your approach to stock investing is to hold stocks for extended periods either for their dividend yield or anticipated long-term growth, then the purchase of options probably doesn't mesh with your objectives (except for sophisticated hedging uses). The "writing" of options (the opposite of buying an option) can be employed in a conservative, yield-oriented course of investment, but option writing typically involves considerable stock turnover for which some investors may not be attuned.

In other words, look out for trap doors, deadfalls, spring guns, and elephant pits.

The CBOE also cautions that "an option is a 'wasting asset' and that, secondary market or not, a call option's value will decline to zero at its expiration unless the price of the under-lying stock is in excess of the option's exercise price." Yes, that's zero. On the other hand, the secondary market, which is the CBOE's innovation, "makes possible at least the partial recovery of the premium paid for an option in instances where it appears, in advance of the option's expiration date, that the price of the stock is not headed for the anticipated rise."

One possible investing maneuver that may be employed is to make a "short sale" of a stock while holding a call option on the stock. (A short sale is selling, by borrowing, a stock you don't own in hopes that its price will drop, at which point you can buy at the lower price, making a profit on the difference. It is, in effect, the other side of a normal "long" stock trans-action.) With such innovations the exchange proclaims the "birth of a distinct new investment medium whose potential uses are limited only by the limits of your imagination."

You've got the idea. If speculation is your thing, the op-tions market will give you plenty of action. But you are buying only options—not the stock itself, which may produce divi-dends and is a solid asset.

Another highly speculative operation is buying contracts for commodity futures. That is, you gamble on the future price of such commodities as wheat, corn, sugar, copper, soybeans, cocoa, even pork bellies. These, of course, are subject to such uncontrollable factors as the wind and weather, insect plagues, droughts, fertilizer and oil shortages, revolutions, and nationalizations of foreign companies in unstable countries. You buy a "futures" contract for delivery of a certain commodity; the contract can be sold before the delivery date. To buy the contract you make a down payment of 10 to 20 percent of the purchase price, plus broker's commissions and clearinghouse fees.

As in the stock options market, one attraction of buying commodity futures is that the down payment is small, and you can either sell your holdings before the delivery date or take delivery, which means you'll have to pay storage costs on the commodity you've bought. Naturally most people sell before delivery, and control the commodity only on paper in hopes of making a profit on its resale if the price of the commodity rises.

Obviously you should know a lot about the commodity you choose to speculate on: how it's produced, the climatic factors, the politics of the country it comes from, the market shifts that might produce a shortage in, say, wheat which would result in an upward trend of prices. For example: Cocoa was in short supply between 1966 and 1969, and the price rose dramatically; in 1973 the Russian wheat purchase shot up the price on those commodity futures. Fine. But predicting such events takes a lot more than a crystal ball or a reliance on hunches. And even then it is, as the securities men say, "shooting the rapids."

If the commodities market seems alluring to you, it's a good idea to practice first on paper, like making mental bets on horse races. Pick out a commodity, pretend to buy futures in it, and see how well you've done. (That way, you'll at least remain decently clothed and fed.) It is enormously challenging to the experienced speculator. Your daily newspaper may, and the *Wall Street Journal* does, carry a complete record of commodity contract prices every day. By studying these tables you can, from day to day, find out how well you would have done had you actually bought or sold a particular commodity contract.

15 /

Of Gold and Gems
and Many Things

So far I have been discussing the more conventional methods of making your money work for you. There remain a number of esoteric bypaths in the marketplace which you may wish to explore, depending on your inclinations and special interests. It's always amazing to me how ingenious human beings can be in conjuring up new ways to create a market and find new possibilities of making their money grow and multiply.

I've heard, for instance, of a group of "little old ladies" who created a unique trading enterprise for themselves: They began collecting jade snuff bottles. The little-old-lady conspiracy expanded to about fifty, and soon they aroused a feverish interest in such objects (though snuff-taking in Beverly Hills has never been a popular addiction). The result was that the ladies controlled a brisk market and found not only profit in the process but the joy of camaraderie.

Most of this chapter won't deal with such exotic commodities as jade snuff bottles, but the possibilities offered require, for the most part, more expertise or special interest than buying stocks and bonds. Some of them, too, are a lot more risky. In any case they will require a considerable amount of self-education and experiment.

GOLD

Just as this book was being written, there was a great golden glimmering on the financial horizon, largely inspired by a change in the federal law that permitted Americans, for the first time in more than four decades, to buy and trade in gold. Starting January 1, 1975, we were allowed to have and hold gold coins and bullion, as well as certificates denoting the ownership of gold.

What happened soon afterward seemed to vindicate the conservative investor's belief that gold is too volatile and unpredictable a commodity to be speculated in by anyone less knowledgeable than one of the gnomes of Zurich, or less well heeled than the ruler of an oil sheikdom on the Persian Gulf. It was widely predicted that gold would rise to $300 or $400 an ounce, once Americans joined the stampede. In expectation of this development, the price on the London exchange rose above $195. Came the New Year dawn, and Americans stayed away from the gold market in droves; the price dropped by $20 an ounce within a week. The boom, at least for the moment, has turned into a bust. Long-range, though, it would not be surprising to see gold at much higher levels if world-wide inflation continues.

It still seems to me that the cautionary words of two of the leading American banks, about a week before gold sales were legalized, not only were wise, but helped to deflate interest in that area. Walter Wriston, the president of the First National City Bank of New York, said that gold was not an "appropriate investment" for most people, explaining, "In the first place you have to have the gold assayed and that's expensive. There would be our service charge and a charge for storing it. If gold were going for $190 an ounce, we'd have to charge you $200."

The Bank of America (headquarters in San Francisco), which, like First National City, decided against dealing in gold, declared in a statement the same day that there would be "minimal" returns for the ordinary investor. "The less you buy," it added, "the greater the drawbacks of gold as an investment. If you buy less than 50 ounces at $180 an ounce, the price must increase to $225 or $240 in order to cover all costs of buying and selling . . . you may have to pay 20 to 30 percent over the quoted market price. The markup covers costs of fabrication, packaging, shipping, handling, storage, insurance, state sales tax, and commissions to distributors and sellers."

What happened to the predicted bonanza for gold traders? Apparently the American public, cynical as it may have become about such pronouncements, believed its government's warnings about the dangers of gold speculation. The federal government legalized the traffic, on the one hand, and officially discouraged participation on the other, warning that gold was a risky investment and that frenzied speculation in the commodity could hinder the country's struggle against recession.

Just as important, perhaps, was tradition. Americans have participated with unholy enthusiasm in gold rushes to such inaccessible places as the badlands of the Dakota Territory, Pike's Peak, Sutter's Creek, and the Klondike. The *getting* of it, however—the adventure, the gamble—was the main thing.

If you've read a little about those nineteenth-century stampedes, you know that the gold-rushers didn't hang on to their gold dust or nuggets any longer than it took to have them assayed and traded in for paper currency. (Or, as my dad recently pointed out: "Isn't it interesting the way the people who buy and sell gold and silver always want to be paid—in *cash.*") The United States has always been a folding-money country, just as some European countries have always been obsessed with gold coinage that could be squirreled away against the next catastrophic war or revolution.

Americans want action for their money. They are fascinated by its self-reproducing qualities if it's put to work. That's another reason the initial response was so lackluster when the U.S. Treasury put up two million ounces of gold for bidding.

It's also true that gold-hoarding goes against the American grain; it fits in better with European pessimism than America's traditional optimism. The fact is that the average American cannot conceive of national defeat and disaster comparable to the collapse of France in 1871 and 1940, or a ruinous inflation such as the one that wiped out the middle class during Germany's Weimar Republic in the 1920s. Zooming gold prices are bad news, as one bullion dealer observed, while "low prices signify trust and friendship."

One of the reasons gold prices soared initially was consumer fear that the dollar was about to be substantially devalued. Panic does cause prices to rise (or drop), but it should be viewed as a temporary phenomenon. One needs to look for more solid factors, such as usage and scarcity.

Then, too, there are less abstract considerations than the impact of gold trading on the American psyche. The chance, for one, of being victimized by a revival of the old gold-brick swindle.

The Federal Trade Commission warns that

the purchase of an investment in gold is a potentially fertile area for unscrupulous promoters and fraudulent schemes, particularly in view of the inflationary state of the economy and the fascination that surrounds gold. Moreover, the price of gold is often dictated by speculative interests and is subject to significant and rapid fluctuations.

Other experts have warned that an adulterated gold bar is hard to detect, even for an expert, without scientific equipment.

The advantage of gold buying, of course, is its aura of solidity and permanence. Gold prices may go down, but you've always got your coins or bullion or whatever; a 15-million-Reichsmark loaf of bread holds no terrors for the gold investor.

The disadvantages, to most Americans, are more numerous:

1. Gold is just another commodity, objectively viewed.

You gain if the price rises. But meanwhile it isn't earning anything for you, it pays no interest or dividends. It may be a hedge against economic catastrophe, but not against creeping inflation.

2. You have to pay a commission on every transaction, whether buying or selling.

3. If you are sensible, you will have your gold assayed before completing any purchase. That costs between $30 and $100 for each sample.

4. You have to pay for its storage (unless you are unwise enough to bury it in your back yard) and also for its insurance.

5. The gold market is highly erratic. Many American experts believe that it is way overpriced (though many of them have been wrong before). If you had bought gold at the one-time United States established price of $42.22 an ounce and sold it in today's market, you could have cleared a profit of up to 400 percent. That statistic is what keeps the gold dealers and speculators singing their siren songs.

But the day of those spectacular rises is probably past. One economist seems to have summed up the realities of the gold market in two sentences: "The time to have bought gold has passed. It is no longer a good buy."

Now that I've said all this and you're still interested in gold, use these caution signs to guide your travels. Wear your gold bangles and necklaces with flair—you could always sell them in a pinch—but *don't* count on a profit on gold.

COLLECTING

Many women have found this area both fascinating and profitable. As everyone knows, the price of art objects and antiques rose to new heights during the lush prosperity of the past two decades. Jewelry, too, has exercised its traditional fascination: a sparkling three-carat diamond (the size more adaptable for resale in any market) possesses far more glamour for many women than money in the bank; and you can put together an exciting collection of semiprecious stones for both pleasure and profit. You needn't have only Chinese jade, for instance; how about tourmalines or garnets? One woman I know judiciously built a collection of antique amber pieces that tripled in value in less than ten years. All these things, like gold, are something to have and hold, come what may—and there's the added fillip in that you can *enjoy* using them and looking at them at the same time you view them as investments.

Collecting in these areas does not require a large initial cash investment so much as a solid level of expertise, sustained enthusiasm, and above all an ability to foresee that an object or style not yet popular is nonetheless likely to become so. A young interior decorator in New York collected Aubrey Beardsley prints long before the revival of interest increased their value; she also began to develop an interest in art deco a good ten years ago, collecting, for very little outlay then, furniture and fabrics and pieces of sculpture entirely as a hobby. What she was doing was betting on her "eye"—anticipating that the art deco lines would eventually fit in with the tastes and moods of today's women. She was right: Recently she was offered $8,000 for a piece of chrome sculpture she had bought for less than $2,000 several years before.

Another point to remember is that the number of fine antiques (like pieces of fine art) is steadily diminishing. It is a closed field in that sense—which means that their value must of necessity increase. And while antiques fare best in boom years, there are always the wealthy and discerning in any period who will pay good prices for beautiful objects in a thousand and one fields.

What you need to do is develop a specialty, to become if you can *the* expert in a certain area, however limited. By selecting a field or period *before* it has become fashionable or chic, developing a specialty in depth, picking up for relatively little money pieces that possess beautiful lines and a certain innate elegance, and hanging on to them, you may very well find that your collection will be worth a good deal in a few years. It is, after all, the timeless you are after—and *you* want to recognize it before others do.

In the mid-1950s a young New York couple asked a friend, an antique dealer, to bring back for them several British officers' campaign chests (*circa* 1814) on his next trip to London. They liked their clean simplicity of line, the mellow wood, the beautiful flat brass handles and handsome fittings; and the fact that they could be divided in two, or combined as living space dictated, made them ideal for apartment and condominium living. The dealer brought them several, at $75 apiece, saw that his friends were right, and brought over a boatload of such chests. The result was a demand for a "new" classic. The couple's original campaign chests are worth $2,000 to $3,000 in the open market today.

Many women have realized a handsome profit through choosing small objects of unusual rarity, unique within a given area but not expensive, such as old tortoise-shell boxes. A collection, as opposed to a single item, begins to have value. A retired schoolteacher developed a passion for (and a superb knowledge of) antique keys from early American, Tudor, and Valois days—elegant little works of art that now are worth ten times the $20 and $40 she paid for them.

Another advantage to collecting on your own lies in the fact that you can pursue it in your spare time. The personal secretary to a prominent Wall Street broker began to collect chess sets of all kinds—ivory, jade, ebony, lemonwood, soapstone, carved in various styles—not simply because she liked to play chess (she did), but because she was certain there would be a surge of popular interest in the game. She is now realizing a small fortune on the collection she began so modestly.

Actually, most women have a special knowledge in many of these areas without ever realizing they do. China and silver and linen were in women's domain from time immemorial —you have only to make them work for you. Who would have thought that the plain, rugged old willow pattern and ironstone ware of grandmother's day are now feverishly sought-after collector's items? Their cleanness of line, charm, and functional design made them endure. Are you excited by Haviland, Wedgwood, Spode, Limoges? Fortunes have been made in them, and in pressed or Sandwich glass, old silver, pewter. (It's much sounder, for instance, to invest in one fine piece of Georgian or period silver, which will always command an excellent resale price, than in factory-made sterling, which has a poor resale value.)

Quilts, as everyone knows, have turned into a tremendous investment, with the revival of interest in colonial and frontier designs. Paisley shawls have proved profitable, and so have rattan and cane furniture, whale-oil lamps, tea tins, and japanned or lacquered canisters, to name only a few specialties. You have only to find what will be the ruling passion of tomorrow.

Here again, the watchword is: *Do your homework*. Prepare yourself carefully. Before buying *anything* you should attend auctions at the most reputable galleries, annotating your catalog with the prices individual items have brought—and you should save those catalogs for future reference. Go to lectures in your field of venture, read in depth, make frequent and careful tours of museums, fit visits to collectors or dealers in your chosen field into vacation trips. Cultivate, if possible, the curators who will make the fashions of tomorrow.

Old bookstores can be absolute gold mines of information and discovery. A children's book illustrator accidentally unearthed some old whaling prints in a bookstore near Sag Harbor, Long Island (once a whaling port), and became so excited that she began to collect prints exclusively on whales. She now owns one of the most distinguished, and valuable, collections of its kind in the country. And a Philadelphia housewife uncovered a sheaf of original Hogarth and Cruikshank prints tucked away in a moldy atlas—a find that launched her on a fascinating voyage of collecting. Original prints, antique maps, and rare books have their fascinations, too, and possess a solid resale value for the knowing. In fact, collecting is probably the only activity in the world that combines pride of possession and the exhilaration of making money with that utterly unique thrill of discovery. There, in that dusty, moth-eaten old shop, there may be an inlaid cribbage board, a Currier and Ives or Thomas Hart Benton print, a Roper serving spoon—and only *you* appreciate its value at this moment, and its value for the future. That is the magic of collecting.

And there is still another incentive. Collectors, like sailors, recognize each other the world over; specialists are drawn to kindred spirits with similar enthusiasms and expertise. Those who collect things more often than not find themselves moving in the company of the wealthy, the perspicacious, the adventuresome, the youthful of spirit. Such encounters invariably make life richer, more enjoyable in a thousand ways. If collecting is work—and it is, and should be, if you want to succeed at it—it is work with an uncommon amount of pure enjoyment and adventure wrapped up in it.

"INSTANT COLLECTIBLES"

Collecting areas such as these require so much special knowledge that it would be impossible to attempt to cover them all in this survey. There is a new field called "instant collectibles," however, that bears examination. Despite the deepening recession at the end of 1974, there was a rush to buy such objects as limited-edition coins, medallions, bars, and plates fashioned from silver. Most such items, unlike established or currently fashionable art and antiques, are in a relatively modest price range. They also offer an aura of permanence and a possibility (not very large) of speculative profit.

"Instant collectibles" proved so popular in the past year or two that they are flooding the market at an estimated rate of a thousand new limited editions yearly—and a glut on the market seems likely. Part of the allure was the fact that a limited edition plate designed by Norman Rockwell sold new for $125 in 1970 and now is being offered at $450.

Experts in the field, including insurers of personal property with a necessarily keen eye for actual value, say there are good reasons for being wary of buying limited-edition silver, among them: The markup on such items is unusually high, upward of 240 percent. The widely advertised collectibles are often incorrectly appraised; that is, at much more than their true market value. Nor is there an established market for resale of collectibles; you'd have to find a buyer on your own. And a lot of fraudulent offerings have appeared on the market, replicas of notable original editions sold as the real thing.

If you buy such plates or medallions, you should do so for their decorative value more than in any hope of gaining a future profit.

Finding sales outlets for your acquisitions will require ingenuity and the same kind of diligence and imagination you will have brought to collecting itself. As you build your collection, you should maintain up-to-date lists of the names and addresses of other collectors *in your area* who specialize in similar objects or fields. Such a list forms an invaluable reference if you suddenly need or want to sell either the whole collection or part of it. Other specialists will of course already know its value, and you can unload it more quickly and advantageously to those who share your particular enthusiasm. Then, too, you should maintain an *updated* list of dealers from whom you've bought. They, too, will form an outlet for resale. And of course there are always the prestigious auction houses such as Sotheby, Parke Bernet. If you have a particularly fine collection, they will evaluate it and offer it for sale. For small items or collections you can always advertise in *Antiques, Yankee,* and similar periodicals.

If you collect prints or paintings, you will soon know the dealers who are most likely to resell individual objects. The important point is keeping up-to-date files. Local museums can also be exceedingly helpful. Make friends with the curators, keep in touch with them; they will give you excellent advice about reselling if and when the need arises. Obviously your local antique shops are useful, but you should plan to sell on a more sophisticated level if you can.

Collecting in itself is fun; and it can be profitable, too.

16 /

Real Estate:
Woman's Realm

If there is one area of investment for which a great many women have a special, built-in affinity, it is real estate. I suppose it goes back to our basic nest-building obsession. Early on, I seriously considered becoming a real estate broker like other women who have turned their concern for home-building and homemaking into something beyond emotional satisfaction. Some center their careers in real estate; others use it as their primary pattern of investment.

Property is capital. Real estate is basic, the oldest invest-ment medium. As long as man has been more or less civilized, he has owned land and built dwellings on it.

And land has one unique characteristic that distinguishes it from other forms of investment. There is a limited supply of this commodity, which cannot be increased by any effort on man's part (other than such marginal operations as landfill or draining swamps). As Will Rogers said of land, "They ain't making it any more." Accordingly, as the population increases and the demand for land and property just as in-evitably keeps pace, real estate prices can be expected to rise in the long run.

You may already have some experience in real estate dealing, especially if you own your own house. If so, you will have experienced one of the most important and appealing elements of real estate, which is referred to as "leverage." In real estate terms, leverage means the ability to control a sizable amount of property for a very small capital outlay. A more direct example of this is the fact that most real estate can be purchased for a relatively small percentage of the overall cost of the property, generally in the 15 to 35 percent range. This, however, depends on how tight the money supply is. The balance of the purchase price is carried by a mortgage or trust deed held by a bank or some other lending institution. (A trust deed is an instrument by which legal title to real estate is conveyed to a third party to be held in trust for a lender until the debt secured by the instrument is paid. It is, in effect, a mortgage with three parties: the borrower, the lender, and the trustee.)

Customarily these loans are repaid in equal monthly installments, often for 20 to 30 years, at a fixed interest rate. (Variable interest rates are now being considered, whereby your interest rates could vary with the fluctuation in the cost of money.) This home-financing structure has enabled millions of Americans to own their own homes and produced one of the most phenomenal developments in the American economy. It also enlivens the possibilities for women interested in entering the real estate business.

Homeownership has a number of economic advantages in addition to the emotional satisfaction of establishing yourself on your own piece of dirt. In addition to leverage, the tax laws have been written to favor the homeowner in that all interest paid on the mortgage is tax-deductible. Since World War II, too, the value of such investments has in the majority of cases steadily risen (or appreciated) in value, in accordance with Will Rogers' dictum.

Richard Gibson, an expert in real estate investment whom I recently interviewed, cautioned against "emotional involvement" when you venture into homeownership. "The most important investment most people make in their lives is in buying a house. And they make that investment from a purely emotional point of view. Many people buy houses that really aren't worth the purchase price because they buy them to keep 'forever.'

"This is a fallacy, because statistics show that the average house turns over once every eight years. There are exceptions to that, of course. But when you buy a house you should plan on how you're eventually going to get rid of it. You have got to think the thing completely through. You must say, 'Sure, everything is going to fall in place, and I am going to live in this house the next hundred years'—but what happens if something changes? What if I have to get rid of the house? Will I have so overimproved it that I'll lose a lot of money on it? Maybe the price you had to pay for your dream house was worth it to you. If so, you have to consider any loss the price you had to pay for a little extra enjoyment."

A woman buying a house on her own, Gibson says, should be careful to lay down ground rules for herself. Spend no more than one-fourth of your income annually on the property—that is, on the monthly payments to the mortgage holder, your taxes, insurance, and upkeep. The total of all that on a yearly basis should be equivalent to 25 percent of your annual income. Gibson also passed on to me an excellent suggestion to "set yourself an absolute dollar limit" when shopping for a house or income property in advance. If you start looking at an $80,000 house when you can realistically afford the payments only on a $50,000 house, you will only disappoint yourself from the very beginning and even be tempted to stretch your resources beyond the limits you can sensibly maintain.

He also cautions against such minor but costly items as the "impound accounts" required by many institutions that finance home buying. Such an account, he explained, works like this: "The bank requires that you pay the principal and interest on a monthly basis. But taxes and insurance are paid on a semiannual or annual basis. So a lot of banks and lending institutions will require that you pay them an estimated amount to cover such payments. This will be placed in a non-interest-bearing account. You send your tax bills to the bank at the end of the year and they pay them out of your impound account."

Gibson recommends that you arrange instead an interest-bearing savings account in which you and the bank are joint proprietors, but from which you can't withdraw without their approval.

"Banks and other lending institutions will try to fight you on that point," he says, "because all financial institutions like funds on deposit which they don't have to pay interest on. Like your checking account. They will give you a free checking account and things like that, but they have the advantage of using that money without paying any interest on it. The same thing is true with impound accounts."

Homeownership has often led women down adventurous bypaths and into the volatile sphere of real estate investment. One interest evolves into a larger one. Success stories involving women and real property abound.

One of my favorites in this area is the story of how Pat Martin, whose real estate operations have boosted her into the $250,000 to $300,000 net-worth category, awakened to opportunity. Years ago, when she was responsible for the rearing of her son (then two years old), she had to go apartment-hunting.

"My son was with me," she recalls, "and the rental agent turned and said, 'Is this yours?' and I said, 'Yes, this young man is mine.' He said, 'We don't rent to children.'

"This came as a rude awakening to me, that in looking for a place to live, as basic a thing as can be, you are dependent on someone else, you're at their mercy. If you had a child or a dog in those days—I think it has changed a great deal since—you were entirely dependent on someone else's understanding attitude.

"And I made up my mind then that I would never in my

life become dependent on anyone else for anything. So I determined that several things were necessary.

"First, we had to have a roof over our heads. I had a job at the time, but my income was barely enough to keep body and soul together, or so it seemed. Then I discovered that actually I had money to spend on other things, that I just had to rearrange my values a little."

Pat, who had come into a small inheritance, combined that with a small loan from her mother to make the down payment on an apartment building. "This assured me that I wouldn't be beholden to anyone else for anything so far as a roof over my head was concerned. We could have a dog, we could do as we pleased because we owned the place. That put me in control. Then I could determine who was going to have the other apartments in the building, without restrictions on dogs or children. I was in the driver's seat for the first time in my life."

She began saving money from various sources and "eventually got to the point where I had enough money for other investments, which were really in the low thousands. In fact, when I made my first investment I didn't know how I was going to meet the obligations on the apartment building.

"But buying that property was my first real step toward independence."

Pat Martin also bought a house when she discovered she could meet all its obligations by renting it out. The rent covered payment on the mortgage, utilities, and taxes. As those obligations on the house were paid off, it also provided the money for her to buy a new car, and she was on her way to real estate operations on a much larger scale.

On the East Coast we have the example of Ms. Pat Fernandez, a multimillionaire real estate and bakery company owner, whose brief and brilliant career also testifies to women's affinity for real estate. She is thirty years old, a widow with three small children—and she controls some $8 million worth of New York property.

How did an early high school dropout achieve so much success in such a short time? The key to success, she says, is "to find your niche—what you do best—and exploit it. Some people think 'exploit' is a dirty word. I don't think so. It's the only way a person can develop his or her full potential."

After experiencing difficulties with the hiring rules of the labor unions, she became a strong believer in that sector of the women's movement concerned with placing females in jobs formerly considered male domains.

Ms. Fernandez left high school at the age of fourteen and headed for Manhattan with $300 she had saved from baby-sitting chores. She went to work part time for a real estate firm, "did some selling and leasing for my boss, and learned about bookkeeping." She made $20 a week, "barely enough to keep going. I kept up contact with my family back on Long Island but I was determined not to go back home."

By the time she was eighteen, she had begun earning some larger commissions on property transactions, though she wasn't old enough to obtain a real estate license. With her savings from those commissions she was able to lease and sublet several small residential properties in Manhattan on her own. When she reached twenty-one she passed the examination for her realtor's license and from then on, as she puts it, "things snowballed."

Two years later that "snowball" represented holdings of more than a million dollars. Ms. Fernandez had caught the crest of the boom in Manhattan real estate and was riding it more successfully, as it turned out, than some magnates who gambled for hundreds of millions in glass skyscrapers and found themselves overextended.

At twenty-three she met Frank Fernandez, a middle-aged man who operated a small bakery on the Upper East Side and owned about 15 Manhattan properties as a sideline, when she tried to sell him one of her apartment houses. Instead of her talking him into buying the property, *he* talked *her* into marriage. Fortunately Fernandez understood how much her business career meant to her. They worked together to build up his high-quality bakery and her mini-empire of real estate.

Two years ago Fernandez was killed in an automobile accident, leaving all the responsibility of their holdings to her. She not only manages the thirty apartment buildings she owns, but is slowly expanding the bakery's wholesale operations to include restaurants, hotels, and airlines.

What's fascinating—and significant—about these two stories is that both Pats started out with very little in the way of capital, and a great deal in the way of brains and energy.

Real estate may be your thing; this will be particularly true if you like the idea of working with something visible and tangible, something less abstract than a stock certificate, less exhausting (in my opinion) than starting your own business.

As in other endeavors, it is absolutely necessary to educate yourself in the field. Burn that midnight oil. Read up on the subject, take a course in real estate management. Or, if you're well heeled, engage the services of a professional real estate analyst (not a broker). The field of real estate is complex; the legal aspects alone demand careful study. A professional approach is needed even if you *don't* intend to acquire a realtor's license and start up your own agency.

At the very least, you should consult an attorney specializing in real estate—one who has no financial interest in whether you buy or don't—before making any investment. If you are interested in getting an appraisal on your property, there is a professional organization, similar in function and stature to that of CPAs, called MAIs. They are members of the American Institute of Real Estate Appraisers and can be contacted in cities throughout the United States. The MAIs (Members Appraisal Institute) are highly qualified individuals who are trained to appraise all types of property from raw land to skyscrapers. Getting this type of appraisal is particularly valuable for tax purposes, for resale purposes, as well as when you are deciding to make a purchase.

If you go into real estate for investment purposes, you'll probably be interested mainly in income property; that is, structures that can be rented to people for homes or businesses, thus providing you with a regular monthly income. The purchase of "raw" land—undeveloped, usually remote from towns or cities, without water mains or electricity—is not generally advantageous, unless you can afford to have your money tied up for a time. There are several reasons for this. Chief among them is the fact that you have to pay for the land without receiving any "offsetting" income. Such land can suddenly become valuable, but it is a highly speculative investment and in recent years both individuals and some large companies have been badly burned. Raw land isn't worth much unless it has some quality attractive for vacation or retirement homes or is close to an expanding population center.

The key to raw land is the price at which you buy it, the plan for improvement, and your financial staying power. In the early 1900s there was a substantial land offering on the East Coast advertised as beach-front property. The going price was around $20 an acre, on easy payment terms. Everything was going beautifully until one of the new landowners went down to view his property and found that it not only was ocean front, but was in fact swampland. The word got out and the offering was soon hailed as a major land swindle. As the years went by, people sold the land at great loss in an effort simply to get rid of it. If you're wondering where this tale is leading, let me hasten to tell you that fifty years have passed and that same swampland is today called Miami Beach, where a front foot of high-rise beach property can hardly be bought at *any* price. If you'd been an owner and had held that land over those fifty years, you would have multiplied your investment 1,000 times over.

A college professor bought several acres of undeveloped shore-front land on the Maine coast, now worth four times what she paid for them five years ago—and there are very, very few Wall Street wizards who could match that rate of profit, even in the go-go years. Another rewarding enterprise can be found in arranging the purchase of relatively large tracts of vacationland by private corporations of people with shared interests. Squam Lake, New Hampshire, Blowing Rock, North Carolina, and Tashmoo Inlet, Martha's Vineyard, are examples of places where entrepreneurs put together immensely attractive land and people who were seeking a new recreational life style.

There *are* fortunes to be made in undeveloped tracts of land. But you must gain precise knowledge of the entire area as well as the real estate in question, and you must be willing to sit on your purchase for quite a while if you have to.

Another important point Gibson passed on to me was that before you go into any real estate investment (in fact, *any* investment), it is imperative that you know how you are going to get into it as well as out of it. By this he means knowing how you're going to buy it, under what conditions, and how you will take title. And, most importantly, how you plan on disposing of it.

Let's take up the most common form of real estate investment, apartment houses.

Often the buyer of such income property will choose to occupy one of the apartments herself, and that's not a bad idea—the closer watch you keep on your investment, the better. The success of such a venture depends on whether the return on the investment is as large as the investor expected it to be when she bought it. That return is, simply, the margin between total rental payments and the cost of owning and maintaining the apartment house.

An all-inclusive mathematical analysis of apartment-house operation is beyond the scope of this book, but here are a few principles that might serve as guidelines if your interest lies in this area. (Naturally you should supplement this by studying any of a number of books available on apartment-house investment.)

One of the greatest hazards of such an operation, aside from having it located in a declining neighborhood, is a high vacancy rate. Before buying any such property you should check its rental records and determine the turnover in rentals—if rapid, why?—and question the tenants as to their satisfaction with their accommodations. In all cases you must assume a certain vacancy factor, usually at least 5 percent, as part of the normal state of things. If a real estate broker tries to tell you that the vacancies average much less than 5 percent, you should assume that he is probably being less than truthful.

In my interview with Pat Martin she stressed the importance of negotiating discounts on the many supplies and furnishings needed in operating an apartment house. Whittling down the dealer's markup on such items will often make a large difference in the profit of your operation.

"For example," she told me, "when you buy anything in a paint store you have to ask for the apartment owner's discount. When they ask how many apartments you have, take a number from one to twenty. Say sixteen. (They don't ask to see the tax bills.) This also applies to something like buying a stove. Many of these are fair-trade items. Sometimes you can get an off-brand that is equally as good as those that are fair-traded. Whatever you buy, you have to negotiate the price. One gallon of paint. One refrigerator. Anything."

Dealers are willing to go along with such discounts because of the prospective business, in volume, you'll presumably bring them. Or, as Pat Martin explained, "If you have ten apartments, you are going to buy ten refrigerators. You don't buy them all at once because they don't all have to be replaced at once. They are purchased at different times. Out of fifteen water heaters, for example, you might have eight go out in one year and the other seven over a period of years. If they come up with the right price this time, they might get invited to the dance the next time, and they know this. But you have to identify yourself in order to get the discount."

Another factor is the expense of maintenance, which depends in part on the age of the apartment house and the state in which it was previously maintained. Property always has to be maintained: walls painted, plumbing repaired, carpets replaced, wiring redone. And you should provide for such expenses beforehand, whether you manage the place yourself or have someone else do it. In addition to such expenses you should figure in your time, which could be devoted to some other profitable endeavor. You'll be occupied with paying for utilities, rubbish collection, landscape work, personal property taxes, real estate taxes—and this should all be figured as a cost factor.

The *cash flow* is the most important criterion of real estate management. This can be defined as the gross rentals, minus the vacancy factor, minus operating expenses, minus payments (if any) on the mortgage principal and interest. Your return is the annual cash flow divided by the down payment you made on the property. This figure normally should be about 10 percent, based on realistic assumptions regarding the vacancy rate and the cost of maintenance.

If you succeed in finding income property that will provide you with a 10 percent return on your investment, you will learn that with wise management such an enterprise will have two considerable advantages:

As a tax shelter. In a typical apartment operation, the depreciation and interest payments are tax-deductible; a good part of the cash flow, if not all of it, will be tax-sheltered. This means, in turn, that your 10 percent return on investment is roughly equal to the 15 to 20 percent you would have to earn on stock investments to gain the same after-tax effect. As always, the tax laws are quite complex and require expert advice before taking action.

As a hedge against inflation. It's a first-rate barrier against rising prices and cheaper money. If you're like most people who own and manage income property, a large part of your investment is borrowed money, repayable at a fixed rate over a determined number of years. Thus as the dollar gets cheaper your payments will be made in dollars that have decreased in real value. This is in accordance with one of the maxims of inflation-fighting: Incur as much debt as possible (up to a certain point and not, of course, personal debt) because the debt will be repaid with cheaper dollars.

To quote Richard Gibson: "You will find the predominance of wealth of the world can be traced to real estate. It's the safest investment you can make, provided it's carefully chosen. No matter how badly you get burned in a real estate deal, if you have staying power, inflation will eventually bail you out." Gibson believes that the primary reason for investing in real estate today is as a hedge against inflation; secondarily, to ensure that "at some point downstream that you have something to generate cash for your retirement years."

There is another hedging aspect to income-producing property: As inflation worsens you'll be able to raise your rents (unless you operate under rent controls set up by the city, or state or federal rent controls which could be reinstituted at any time.) Rents should increase at a faster rate than the growth of your operating expenses. Your cash flow and net income will rise. Those figures, in turn, will increase the value of your property when and if you decide to sell it.

Selling income property is usually advisable when depreciation no longer provides a shelter for your income. Some of the gain or appreciation (the difference between what you sold the property for and what you paid for it) will be subject to long-term capital gains treatment, which means that the taxes should be substantially lower than on ordinary income. Without going into all the technicalities of the very complex tax law in this area, you will generally receive favorable tax treatment on your real estate holdings from the tax-shelter aspect while you are holding it and the partial long-term capital gains treatment when you sell it.

But there is a negative side, too. Often it's difficult to locate an apartment house or other income-producing property on which a small investor can afford the down payment. In such cases you may well find it necessary to join forces with a friend or associate to swing the deal.

If you're in the financially undernourished category, you might want to consider "fix-up property." That is, you buy a house or apartment building in run-down condition, at a modest price, and renovate it. But be warned: *Never* buy run-down property in a deteriorating neighborhood. No matter how beautifully you renovate it, its value will sink along with its neighbors'. Many people have bought such property in a desirable neighborhood and managed to resell at a handsome profit after earning income during the period of ownership. It helps, of course, if you're knowledgeable, to have expert advice about necessary repairs to the building.

The other type of income property is industrial and commercial. Such property is often expensive, an impossible area for the small investor unless she pools her resources with those of other people.

Commercial and industrial property can provide a strong and steady source of income. All-important is the quality of tenant to whom you lease the property. Ideally, the tenant should be a triple-A-rated corporation (one with the highest credit standing) and the lease should be on a net-net-net basis. This means that the tenant, not the owner, pays for all expenses attendant to the property including taxes, repairs, maintenance, and upkeep; in short, everything except the mortgage payment. The owner has neither expenses nor management problems to contend with. The risk is low and the precalculated return on the investment may be greater than that of other forms of real estate operation. It also lends itself to absentee ownership; you don't have to keep a watchful eye on the property.

For these reasons, mortgage loans can be made on commercial/industrial property, particularly if the tenant is a good credit risk. A long-term lease can have the same inflation-hedging and appreciation advantages that apartment houses often do, particularly by providing in the long-term lease that the annual rental is increased in direct ratio with the Cost of Living Index or some other fairly accurate economic indicator such as the GNP Deflator (Gross National Product Deflator).

Now for the negative side of commercial/industrial property. One is that the improvements or structural changes made by the lessee will tend to be single-purpose. Suppose you lease your building to a fast-food chain or a similar franchise operation. You would have great difficulty in re-leasing the property without making expensive alterations to the interior and exterior of the structure. A less dramatic example might be a tenant engaged in industrial manufacturing who would want improvements on the building—improvements that might be of no value to the tenant who succeeds him. This is the great drawback to industrial/commercial property ownership. Being aware of that, you should demand of your first tenant a commensurate return on the risk you take, or require the tenant to make any required changes himself and leave them in place when he gives up the lease. This is, in fact, a clause usually included in such leases.

If you have, say, a 10,000-square-foot building for assembly or light industry of some kind, it will often attract entrepreneurs without much capital or a high credit rating. Here you're taking the risk that they will fail before the expiration of the lease and leave you with the problem of a long vacancy during which you try to find another tenant. A safer investment, probably, is the recently popular mini-warehouse in which you rent space to householders for possessions they can't find room for in their homes or garages.

Location is all-important in any real estate development. Whether it's an apartment house or industrial/commercial property, you should consider such paramount factors as the accessibility of public transportation, the declining or advancing status of the district, the incidence of crime in the neighborhood, the availability of housing nearby if it's an industrial building. You also must possess staying power. By that I mean you should have calculated your financial position carefully enough so that you can be sure you'll be able to keep up the mortgage payments even in periods of adversity, to survive even if you run into an increased vacancy rate. If you have enough capital or income to get over the rough spots, you'll find that time often favors the investor who is farsighted enough to hang on to his property, gradually improve it, and profit from the long-run upward trend of real estate values.

Another important factor is knowing how to negotiate (and not being diffident about doing so). We've been over this ground earlier and I won't belabor it here. You can be sure that people with real estate to sell will be asking quite a bit more than they really expect to get. If you pay the asking price without at least trying for a lower price, you are lacking in common sense, or at least common knowledge. Pat Martin cites the case of a "very unsophisticated couple" who several years ago were interested in a house for which the asking price was $47,000. "They did not know that it was customary to negotiate or that they should have offered forty thousand to forty-two-five and induce the sellers to come down to around forty-five thousand. So their inability to negotiate cost them at least several thousand dollars. Nobody has ever come along and handed me that much money for nothing. They acted as they did not out of stupidity, not because they were young, but out of lack of knowledge."

17 /

The Tax Man Cometh

It's only fitting that my last chapter be devoted to that sometimes menacing bureaucracy, the Internal Revenue Service. Nothing is certain but death and taxes, as folk wisdom has it. But taxes come first. They have to be lived with, and understood. Coping successfully with them can often mean the difference between profit and loss on your year's operations. And they have to be dealt with on a continuing basis, not just as something to be fretted over the night of April 14. The tax laws are constantly being changed by Congress, and the revisions must be noted and, if possible, taken advantage of *as they are made*. Many people discover they've been overly generous to Uncle Sam only when it's too late.

You can keep up with the ebb and flow of tax legislation through a number of softcover books such as the *Prentice-Hall Federal Tax Handbook* and the *J. K. Lasser Tax Institute,* which are issued annually in new editions. They will provide specific ways of obtaining legal tax savings as well as defining areas where deductions cannot be taken. You should also read and thoroughly understand the brochure the government sends you with its income tax forms. If it is unclear, don't gloss over it. What you don't understand can cost you money. One place to get help (not the best, in my opinion, but the cheapest) is the IRS, which provides a service on a year-round basis in order to answer your questions. Of course, the closer you get to tax time, the more waiting time is involved in getting information from these offices.

Every year you should take it for granted that the federal tax code resembles that designation "terra incognita" found on some maps, indicating unmapped territory bristling with swamps and quicksand.

Here are a number of brief suggestions regarding income taxes that should be emblazoned on your mind when you sit down to the annual tussle with your conscience, your sense of discretion, and your IRS return.

Don't ever cheat. I italicize this admonition because the money you might save simply isn't worth the sleepless nights it entails or the chance you'll be caught in an audit, with heavy penalties to pay. Besides, "it would be wrong."

Remember: *There is no statute of limitations on tax fraud.* And a fraudulent return is *your fault*—not that of the person who may have filled out your return.

This point made, let me now advise you: Don't be afraid to use every *legitimate* means of lowering your tax within the rules of the tax code. Be aware of the difference between legal *avoidance* and illegal *evasion.* On judgmental issues it is perfectly permissible to give yourself a break—and then pay up if an IRS agent disagrees.

If you're in the 30 percent-plus tax bracket, you should have your returns made out by a tax accountant. Generally he'll save you more—sometimes much more—than the fee involved in retaining him.

Learn the difference between short-term and long-term capital gains, and what that might mean to the amount you'll pay on your income. For example, in order to avail yourself of the long-term capital gains provision, six full months must elapse between your purchase of a capital asset and its resale. (I'll go into that in more detail in a minute.) It's an elementary enough clause, but you'd be amazed at the number of people who've been burned simply through ignorance of it.

It's a fact that income taxes become a thorny problem just when your income rises to the level at which you can consider the possibilities of investing whatever savings or capital you've accumulated. The most basic investment most people make is in purchasing a house. If this is the case with you, you should know that you can count on substantial savings on federal income taxes. For example: You've bought a house costing $35,000. Your down payment is 20 percent, or $7,000. The balance of the purchase price is handled by a mortgage of $28,000. If it's a 25-year mortgage at 8 percent interest, you will be paying $2,594 annually in principal and interest. During the first year, the interest part of your payments will amount to approximately $2,240—all of which is tax-deductible. And the property taxes you pay can also be deducted.

If you are self-employed, you should, if circumstances dictate, take advantage of HR-10, the so-called Keogh plan. This provides, through an act passed by Congress in 1963, for your own retirement fund. Under a recent amendment to the act's provisions, you can set aside 15 percent of your annual income up to $7,500. This amount is deductible from your income tax. Also the tax on any dividends or capital gains or interest received from HR-10 may be deferred while you're accumulating the fund. Any woman who is self-employed should look into the Keogh plan. Keogh investments may be made in open-end mutual funds, annuities, endowment or life insurance contracts, savings and loan certificates, or a series of U.S. bonds authorized for this purpose.

The most important thing about handling your tax problem, which gets bigger and more complex as your wealth increases, is to realize that it can't be deferred until a few days before the deadline. You have to plan, to plot your course ahead of time. You should start tax planning in December for the following year—*16 months* in advance of payment.

If you keep up to date on how much tax you're incurring on your income, you can save yourself money. Then you can take advantage of the fluctuations. For instance, you might cash in your government "E" bonds in a low-income year. These bonds are taxable in the year cashed, or the taxpayer may elect to report the taxable increments for each year as income for that year.

All this is part of your essential record-keeping. You should maintain a running account of your earnings and return on your investments. You should keep copies of everything you send the IRS. It's equally essential to retain all canceled checks. In general, records should be kept for six years after the tax return was or should have been filed, whichever is later.

You must also master the basics of the tax system. For better or worse, they're an integral part of your life; they won't just go away so long as you are producing enough income to be taxed. The whole subject becomes less scary the more you know about it. There are certain angles it might be well to learn more about. That, for instance, you can be penalized if you underestimate your income (as a self-employed person) by 20 percent or more. That it's vital to file an *amended return* if you discover that, knowingly or not, you've cheated the government out of its share. Probably your best safeguard against slipping into trouble with Uncle Sam (next to becoming as expert in the subject as possible) is to have the advice of a good tax accountant on a continuing basis—not merely to fill out your returns but to consult on the best moves to make during the year that will enable you to take full advantage of any possible tax breaks. Finding a good accountant, one with "creative" ideas, can be difficult; most people hear about them from their friends, others have to take their chances with the trial-and-error method. The best source I know is your banker. Unfortunately, there is no rating service for excellence in accountancy, only hearsay.

For those who have started a business on their own or initiated an investment program, there are several areas that must be thoroughly understood.

The first principle is that you should never make an investment decision for tax reasons alone. The two must be kept separate. If a certain stock has appreciated greatly in value since you bought it, don't make the mistake of not taking your profit because you don't want to pay the capital gains tax. This is foolish. As an example, if the stock you bought for $20 three years ago is now selling for $75 and you have no reason to believe it will go higher, sell it and pay for your long-term capital gain of $55. If your tax amounts to $14 (the approximate tax if your normal income tax bracket is 50 percent), be glad you made your after-tax profit of $41 per share.

Whether you're planning to enter the market, own real estate, or start your own business, there are several areas that should be thoroughly understood.

CAPITAL GAINS AND LOSSES

There are important distinctions in the types of gains and losses. A *long-term capital gain* is incurred if you buy securities or real estate and hold them for more than six months before selling them. On this type of transaction you are subject to only *half* the regular tax rates on income (unless you have taken a gain of more than $50,000 or are in a rarefied tax bracket, in which case the rate is higher).

A *short-term capital gain* is one resulting from holding a stock or bond or any kind of property six months or less. You pay the regular tax rate—the same as on any other kind of income—on a short-term gain. Therefore it possesses no tax advantage.

Capital losses are self-explanatory, being the reverse of gains. First, for tax purposes, they must be used to offset capital gains. If you have a net short-term capital loss (after gains have been subtracted), you can apply it against up to $1,000 of ordinary income. Should you have a net long-term capital loss after the subtraction of long-term gains, you can apply *half* of the long-term loss against up to $1,000 of income during that tax year. In succeeding years, a similar amount of the loss can be carried over against future years' capital gains and, when fully applied, against ordinary income up to $1,000 per year.

You should keep a careful running account of purchases or sales of stocks or bonds, noting whether there are long-term or short-term gains involved. And keep equally careful records of sales and purchase dates, especially the confirmation slips issued by brokerages which establish the exact dates of the transactions. They're what the IRS auditor might demand to see.

This is the exact way the IRS measures the six-month holding period that determines whether you've made a long-term or short-term capital gain or loss: The period must be at least six months plus one day to be reckoned long-term. The period begins the day after the purchase date and includes the date of sale. Thus a stock bought on January 15 would be a long-term transaction if it was sold on or after July 16.

In differentiating between tax avoidance and tax evasion, as the IRS certainly does, you should beware of the so-called wash sale. You cannot claim a capital loss on the sale of a stock if within 30 days before or after the sale you purchase the same stock, thus offsetting your sale. You may, however, buy the stock of another company in the same industry without penalty.

Let's say you're attached to our mythical National Electric as an investment, and bought 50 shares several years ago at $50 a share. On November 15 this year you sell the stock, which has declined to $40 a share. That provides you with a $500 capital loss against other income. But suppose that on December 1 the stock has revived, or you become interested in it again for other reasons, and you buy another 50 shares of National Electric. In that case you can't claim a capital loss on the first transaction without incurring the wrath of Internal Revenue. That's a wash sale, which applies only to losses, not gains. If you want to buy into National Electric again, you should wait at least 31 days.

In considering capital gains and losses, expert investors start mulling over their portfolios in the autumn to decide whether to buy or sell certain issues. Many sell weeks or months before the calendar year ends, which means that they can make a calm and rational decision based on the worth of the investment without being unduly influenced by the pressure of the tax deadline.

Less experienced investors, on the other hand, often fly into a panic as the year is ending and scramble to sell stocks

—perhaps unwisely—simply because they want capital losses to offset capital gains they've already taken. The wisest counselors say that *you should never sell a security just to get a tax break.* Your portfolio is more important than your tax position.

Another disadvantage of panicky selling late in the year: You'll often find that the stock market declines just because other people are doing the same thing. You might take a more sizable loss than you want in December, and then find that it costs a lot more to buy back into the market in January.

The name of the stock investment game, after all, is capital gains.

DEDUCTIONS FOR INVESTORS

If you have any sort of investment program going, you can probably claim deductions from your federal income tax on a number of items you may not have considered. Singly they may seem a drop in the bucket, but added together they can result in substantial savings.

You may deduct for investment counseling, for renting the safety deposit box in which your stock certificates are kept, for the expenses of getting to and from your broker's office, for the services of an accountant who handles your investments; you may legitimately claim subscriptions to the *Wall Street Journal* and other such periodicals and market-advice newsletters, any transfer taxes you might pay the state on stock transactions, preparation of your income tax return, and any expenses (telephone, stamps, office supplies) incurred in managing your investments.

TYPES OF RETURNS

Whether you itemize or take standard deductions is something you should decide after figuring it out both ways. Naturally you take the one that will cost you the least.

Usually, if you're married, you'll get a better break by filing a joint return. In some cases, however, it is advantageous to file separate returns. The only way you can find out, though, is by figuring it both ways and adopting the least expensive course.

REAL ESTATE

It's a good thing to remember the advantages of the *installment sale* in dealing with real estate. If you've sold a house and received half the purchase price with a note for the balance, for instance, you'd have to pay taxes on the full amount of the capital gain. But if the down payment is less than 30 percent, it becomes an installment sale and you pay taxes on the capital gain corresponding to each year's pro-rated installment. A considerable saving is the result.

Another tip on real estate: Depreciation can be deducted by the owner or part owner, thus providing a tax shelter. Say you own a $10,000 interest in an income property, on which your share of the depreciation is $1,000. You can deduct that from other income, thereby saving yourself $500 if you're in the 50 percent bracket. But remember that tax shelters aren't a free-lunch counter; many more persons in the past several years have been badly damaged seeking out such shelters as cattle breeding and oil and gas depletion allowances than have made fortunes.

AUDITS

How do audits come about? How do you respond if your taxes are audited? Contrary to current legend, there is no malignant gnome somewhere spinning a roulette wheel lined with all our names. The Internal Revenue Service runs all returns through its computers, and each area of the return is keyed to a percentage of your total income. Your return *may* then be pulled for a closer scrutiny by an agent of the IRS. If that bureau should decide there may be grounds for an audit, they will call you to set up a meeting, either at their local office or at your office or home. (The locale of the meeting is usually determined by where and how voluminous your records are. If the audit is routine, you will probably be requested to go to the IRS office.)

Frequently, they will tell you on the phone what the area in question is. If they don't, by all means ask. That is your right. The IRS *office audit* is called a general office audit. The *home audit* is called a general field audit. On the more complex audits, those involving big money, they may not tell you what area they are looking into. (That's *their* prerogative.)

How should you act? No tricks, sleights, or evasive ploys apply here. Your attitude should be one of full and open cooperation, but not obsequiousness or timidity (unless, of course, you have something to feel guilty about; in which case, my condolences). But if by any chance the agent should prove aggressive or hostile, *don't* try to play his game. Simply break off the meeting and ask to speak with his supervisor; and it might be a good idea to bring someone along with you to the next meeting.

Should you bring a lawyer or your tax person to the first meeting? Probably not, unless you know up front you're going to need one. If you do, don't waste time. Wheel in your professionals at the opening bell and get right down to cases.

In that first meeting, let *them* ask the questions. If you don't have the exact answer to some, don't wing it. Look up the information, or if you can't do that then and there, ask for another meeting.

How often does the IRS collect? Well, how often do cops give tickets? While the IRS *claims* they're not on a quota system, the statistics are grim: 9 times out of 10 they dig out something that will cost you something. You don't have to accept their decision, though; if you've got solid grounds for disagreeing with the agent, you can ask to speak with his supervisor—and if you still can't reach an agreement, you can ask to sit down with *another* supervisor. If the matter is still unresolved after that, your next option is the Appellate Division, which serves as an intermediary between the IRS and the Federal Tax Court. These higher levels of appeal naturally become costly (and they require the preparation of briefs), but in some cases they may be worth the effort.

How many returns are reviewed? Nobody knows for certain, but the best guess is, roughly:

Income	Ratio
Under $10,000	1 out of 100
$10,000–$15,000	1 out of 50
Higher income brackets	Virtually 100% inspection

This means the returns that are called are not necessarily audited. Audits also depend on how busy the IRS happens to be. If they have time on their hands, they do lots of audits; if they're swamped, they have to let a lot of returns slip by. (I wouldn't advise fudging on your return on the chance they might be overworked that week.)

GIFTS AND ESTATE TAXES

Anyone with family responsibilities—and indeed any responsible person—will want to consider these matters.

The federal tax code permits anyone to give $3,000 in cash or stocks or other property each year to any number of people without paying any gift tax on it. Nor do the recipients have to pay income tax on the gifts.

Thus if you had four children you could give each of them $3,000 a year every year. (The IRS, however, can challenge any gift made within three years of the donor's death on the grounds that the gift was made "in contemplation of death.")

If your husband joins in the project, he too can give $3,000 tax-free to any number of individuals. The law also provides that each of you can make a once-and-for-all gift of $30,000 (or $60,000 per couple), the so-called lifetime exemption, aside from the $3,000 annual gifts.

Thus it is possible for you to give away a sizable portion of your estate without incurring a tax liability. It's a good way to provide for your children's education, for instance, by giving them the money *before* they enter college, investing it meanwhile in securities or whatever you choose.

As any probate expert will tell you, estate taxes, which must be paid within fifteen months after death and after other debts and attorneys' fees have been taken care of, can be very high and escalate rapidly if the estate is valued at more than $60,000.

"The power to tax involves the power to destroy," the great Chief Justice Marshall observed in a famous decision—to which a lot of us could murmur, "Amen." Taxes are a continuing burden, and a heavy one, but if you gain an understanding of the system and move within it adroitly, you won't be destroyed. And there's also a quiet gratification involved in feeling yourself to be a productive member of society. Wisely handled, your tax problems can be kept under control—*your* control—and you'll have enough after-tax income to achieve financial independence. *Anticipation* is the watchword here, along with hard-won expertise.

ESTATE PLANNING

If you have been successful or hope to be successful in your investment career, you should consider what to do about your eventual estate. This is especially important if you have the sole responsibility for your children.

For advice in this area, I went to Nancy Boxley Tepper, a Los Angeles lawyer who specializes in estate planning. Many of her clients are retired people, but, she says, "I have a substantial number of clients in their thirties and forties who are concerned that the funds they have built up through good investments and careful income-tax planning will be passed in the event of death to their children or other beneficiaries with a minimum of death expenses." That's the bottom line in the matter of estate planning: minimizing the inheritance taxes and conserving your assets for those you care about.

Ms. Tepper has noted that younger women now are more knowledgeable about a family's finances than the men are. "There has been a kind of shift in responsibility," she remarks. "Among the women in their thirties and forties, they often have a better grasp than the men. With retired couples, involving older women, we set up estate plans under the husband's management so long as he is willing and able. When the man dies, the responsibility goes to a bank because the lady says uh-uh, she can't handle it, John always managed their financial affairs. But among my younger clients it is often the woman who knows they bought an orange grove for exactly this purpose and that this Treasury bill matures on this date. Often I find that professional men don't have the time or inclination to become expert in financial matters, and the women take over in this field."

She herself has an estate plan drawn up so "my very young children would receive what I've built up, eliminating probate costs and substantially reducing taxes. They are what I call 'death taxes.' Many people don't understand this. There are income taxes, and then when you die there are death taxes in addition."

In most states you pay a federal estate tax and a state inheritance tax. "You have various deductions that you can take," Ms. Tepper explains, "funeral expenses, the costs of the last illness, etc. What is left, the net estate, is taxed at a pretty hefty rate. All this is part of planning your financial future. Good planning will result in your children or other beneficiaries receiving as much as possible of what you've built up from a lifetime of effort."

Trusts are an excellent way of guaranteeing such results. This, according to Ms. Tepper, is the way they work: "A trust is an instrument under which legal title is held by one party, the trustee, for the benefit of other parties. A bank can hold assets as trustee for other parties. Or a person can act as trustee for other parties or himself or herself.

"One of the main advantages of a trust is that the property it contains is not subject to probate on the death of the person who forms the trust. If an estate is subject to probate, there will be a delay of about a year before the estate is distributed and there will be statutorily fixed attorneys' fees and court costs."

Much red tape and delay is eliminated by the creation of a trust. The trustee takes over title to your property immediately after your death; there is no probate process to hold up distribution, and the costs of probate are avoided. The initial expense of setting up a trust is, however, larger than merely making out a will. Depending on how complicated it is, a will costs from $60 to $150 in attorneys' fees, Ms. Tepper says. Creating a trust, also depending on its complexity, will cost from $600 to $1,200, but will be more than made up in elimination of probate expenses.

The size of your estate should dictate whether you make out a will or create a trust. "A person with an estate of a hundred thousand dollars or more should opt for a trust," Ms. Tepper believes. "You trade off a few hundred dollars of additional expense for setting up the trust against several thousand in probate costs if you leave your money and property in a will.

"Younger women with small children should consider two factors. First, the appointment of a reliable person as their guardian; second, the creation of a trust that will protect their future, since you wouldn't be leaving your holdings to them outright. You should spell out very carefully at what ages you want the children to receive their shares in your estate, taking into consideration college and medical expenses. If it is a small estate, you may want the remaining funds distributed to the children when they reach twenty-one. If larger, you will probably want it distributed at intervals."

The most common instrument is a "revocable living trust," the provisions of which can be changed at any time.

You have the full use of the money and property it contains during your lifetime and you can change beneficiaries and the amounts they would receive. Naturally you have to pay a full income tax on all its assets. You save on what Ms. Tepper calls the "death taxes."

There are also a variety of "irrevocable trusts," which can result in savings on income taxes. One form of this kind of trust is to set aside income-producing property for ten years, with the income going to your beneficiaries during that period. At the end of ten years, the property reverts to your possession. The tax savings result from the fact that if, for instance, you make your three small children the beneficiaries of the income, they would be taxed at a much lower rate than if it were part of your own income.

The cornerstone of estate planning is your will. For without one, the state where you legally reside will make all decisions on your estate, how it is to be transferred, taxed, and distributed. There is simply no substitute for a will. Perhaps the best advice I can give you is not to attempt to make one up yourself. Turn the problem over to an attorney. The fees for drawing up a will are relatively standard and the complexity of a will varies with the size and complexity of your estate. When discussing your will with an attorney you will need to make the following decisions: Who will your beneficiaries be? You will need to make a list of the various people, whether members of your family or associates or friends, to whom you wish portions of your estate transferred.

The next step is to decide what it is you're going to have transferred. Perhaps the best way to go about this is to use your net worth calculation, which you developed in Chapter 3. It is very important to be thorough in this area and include everything you legally own from stocks, bonds, and real estate to furs, jewelry, and other personal items. You will also want to consider such areas as royalties due you, ownership in companies—whatever. You'll need to determine who the executor of your estate will be and, if you choose, you may decide to have joint executors such as your husband and your child. If it's a particularly complex estate, you might also want to consider specifying an attorney or business associate as executor by name. Another consideration will be the guardians for your children.

Perhaps one of the most important elements of a will is that it needs to be reviewed periodically and changed along with any major changes in your life. For instance, your will, if made up today, may transfer the bulk of your estate to your parents, but if you are to be married in several months you may want to amend your will to transfer the bulk of your estate to your new husband. Wills should also be amended whenever a major property in your will is sold or a new one acquired. Some changes may necessitate the drawing up of an entirely new will. In other circumstances your will may require only a codicil (an amendment). However, it's important to remember that a codicil needs to be both witnessed and legally drawn. If a codicil is added to a will and either not witnessed or not signed or in some other way improperly drawn, it can invalidate your entire existing will. The making of a will is often thought of as something to be done later on in life, but I believe that no matter what age you are, you should have a will if for no other reason than consideration for those people you care about.

A Note from the Author

What I wanted to do most in this book was shatter the phony mystique that has kept women from enjoying the confidence and fun that come with the art of making money. Because making money *is* fun, as I've tried to show—and it's a lot more than that. By becoming financially assertive you will find the key not only to security and independence but to your success as a mature human being. It is your *right* to take control of your financial future. But you will learn that it is a delight, too. Creatively pursued, the money game is indeed the most exciting game of all. Come join those of us who've found that financial awareness has brought a sound and rewarding life style. We did it and so can you.

Now go to it!

—PAULA NELSON
August, 1975

Paula Nelson's pioneering efforts in women's financial awareness have made her a highly visible lecturer and seminar leader at leading universities, civic groups and financial institutions. In keeping with her work to continue education and research, she has formed Joy of Money, Inc. Your questions and comments regarding specific areas of financial interest may be addressed to:

Joy of Money, Inc.
9301 Wilshire Boulevard
Beverly Hills, California 90210